A University for Bristol

F

i

A University for Bristol

An informal history in text and pictures

by Don Carleton

*Knowledge will never hurt us, and whoever lives to see an
University here, will find it give quite another turn to
the Genius and Spirit of our Youth in general. How many
Gentlemen pass their lives in a shameful Indolence, who might
employ themselves to the purpose, were such a Design set
on foot? Learning would flourish, Art revive, and not only
those who study'd would benefit by it; but the Blessing
' would be convey'd to others by Conversation.*

Daniel Defoe 1728

University of Bristol Press

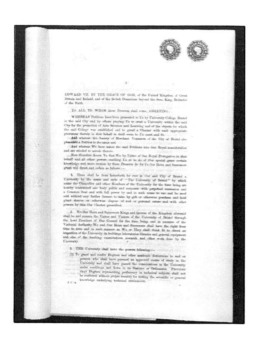

The Charter of the University *is a disappointing document in appearance:* **the Grant of Arms** *from the College of Heralds is much more impressive.*

Contents

Acknowledgments

The University acknowledges with gratitude the contribution made to this book by: the City of Bristol, the Society of Merchant Venturers, the County of Avon Library, the Royal Society, Gill Furlong of the Library, University College, London, the University of Liverpool, the University of Sheffield, the University of Sussex, Sir Vivian Fuchs, the Bristol Old Vic, the BBC, Granada Television, Pressens Bild of Sweden, NASA, the Imperial Group, BVC Ltd of Leatherhead, Cadbury-Schweppes, Victoria and Albert Museum and Henry Willcock & Co Ltd. In particular the University acknowledges a grant from the Alumni Foundation which has assisted publication.

Publishing Data

Published by the University of Bristol Press, 8 Priory Road, Bristol BS8 1TZ. All rights reserved. No part of this publication may be reproduced, stored in a retrieval system or transmitted, in any form, or by any means, electronic, mechanical, photo-copying, recording or otherwise without the permission of the University of Bristol.

ISBN 0 86292 200 3.

First published in 1984.

The views expressed here are not necessarily the views of the University of Bristol.

Set in 11 pt Bembo
by Helen Lamb and Lynn Winstone

Printed by
Gemini Graphics & Print Ltd
Wade Street, Bristol.

Designed by Christopher Matthews.

British Library Cataloguing in Publication Data.

Carleton, Don
 A University for Bristol
 1. University of Bristol – History
 I. Title
 378.423'93   LF65

ISBN 0-86292-200-3

o/c

Preface

This book has been produced to mark the 75th anniversary of the granting of a Charter forming the University of Bristol. Although it lacks the scholarly apparatus of footnotes, references and so on which might be expected to characterise a formal history of the University, it is, nonetheless, based on the sources published and unpublished that a formal history would use. It includes some things which are well established, even commonplace, about the University and some things which are novel; it contains material which is curious and some which is comic; it is rich in pictures and anecdote. It is intended to be a portrait of the University, "warts and all", written and presented in a way which is readily accessible to all readers. It is, in short, an informal history of the University.

The views expressed, the interpretation of men and events are personal and not everyone who has read the documents or who took part in, or remembers, the events described here will agree with my judgements. In preparing the book I have had the help and advice of the Registrar and Secretary of the University, Mr Evan Wright, and of Dr Basil Cottle. They read the manuscript and assisted in the choice of pictures. They drew my attention to errors of commission and omission. Mr George Maby at the University Library also read the manuscript and made, from his great knowledge of the University Archives, further suggestions and corrections. If any errors remain, the fault is mine, not theirs.

I am greatly indebted to Mr Wright, Dr Cottle and Mr Maby and I would like to acknowledge here my gratitude to Miss W. M. Armstead, Miss Margaret Goodbody, Michael and Estelle Morgan, Mr Silvanus Hanbury Aggs, Professor Skemp of the University of Warwick and his sister, Margaret Dawson-Bowling, Professor Peter Fowler, Mr John Bosanko and Mr Michael Pasco for allowing me to reproduce photographs from their family collections. I am grateful too to Gordon Kelsey and his staff at the Arts Faculty Photographic Unit, to Ron Radnedge and Helen Lamb and the staff of the University Printing Unit and to my own staff in the University Information Office for their very great technical assistance in the production of the book. I am grateful too to all the other present and past members of staff, students and employees who gave me their recollections and views of the University. I hope that they, no less than the general reader, will find much to interest them in these pages.

Don Carleton
Bristol 1984

The old Council Chamber: *the ceiling is one of the University's 'hidden' pleasures which few people notice.*

Chapter One

Before the Charter

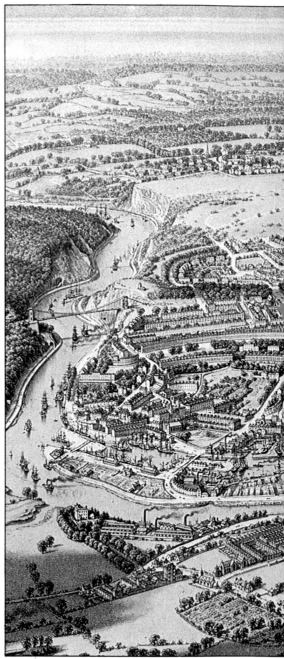

The latter half of the nineteenth century saw a great population increase in Bristol. For the first time Bristol developed residential suburbs. The old prestigious areas in the centre of the city, such as Queen's Square and St Paul's, declined into industrial and commercial use and new middle-class suburbs for the affluent burgeoned in Clifton, Redland and Cotham. The old social cohesion of the city which had seen rich and poor, workplace and home, exist side by side, was being broken. There were evident new social dangers as a man and his master started to live differently and more distantly one from another.

But the latter half of the nineteenth century was also a great age of growth in religious sentiment and the affluent classes who went to live in Clifton, Redland and Cotham recognised a need to help the poorer fellow citizens they left behind. For some middle-class congregations and parishes 'a need to help' meant simple evangelism: the knowledge of the Lord would bring solutions to the problems of drink, poor housing, and poor hygiene. For others, the social problems of the growing city needed a social as well as a religious response: their chosen weapon was education.

Chief among those in Bristol who favoured the educational approach was the Reverend John Percival, headmaster of a newly founded middle-class public school, Clifton College. Percival believed in the need to aspire to a higher civilization, one infused with 'sweetness and light'. This led him to a concern that there should be the widest possible diffusion of educational facilities.

In 1868, when Percival was 34 years old, he founded an Association for the Promotion of the Higher Education of Women. In 1869, he founded an Association for the Promotion of Evening Classes. It was an attempt to meet the needs of the respectable working classes; in Percival's own words, "the clerks, shopmen, artisans and other young men in business". In 1870 he was appointed to be a member of the School Board which was charged under the new Education Act with providing primary school education for all. But another idea was already taking Percival's attention: the creation of a university in Bristol.

Laver's map of Bristol: *an aerial view, drawn and spires of old Bristol to the south.*

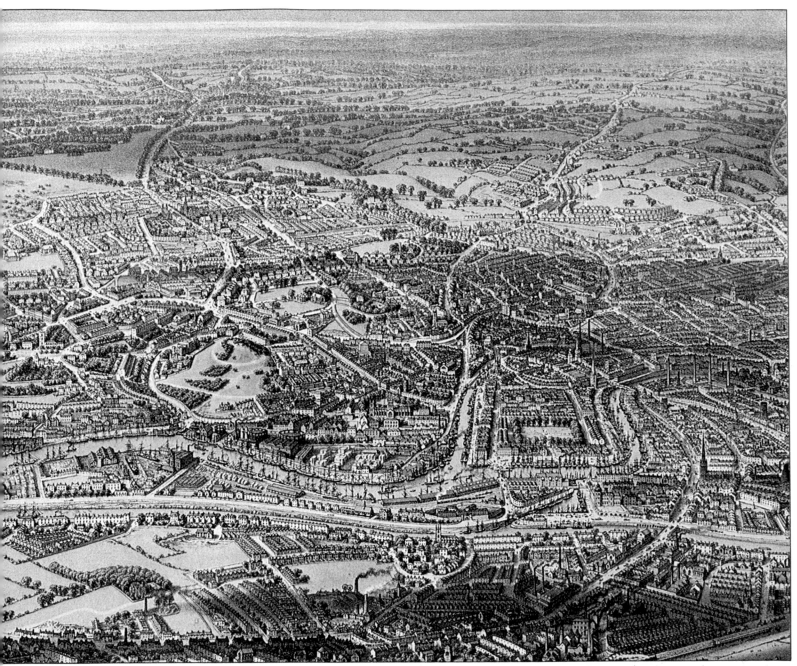

on, it shows the University College of Ramsay's day as an L-shaped structure standing between the new suburbs to the north and the chimneys

The Victoria Rooms. When the inaugural meeting to form the University College was held the building had an open courtyard and a wide road in front of it. Later the City divided the road and created a fine memorial fountain to King Edward VII, the monarch who granted the Charter.

The idea was not a new one. It had been talked about for several years. There was already a movement, especially among the staff of the Infirmary and the General Hospital, to found a College of Science in Bristol. But Percival saw that this movement, if it were to succeed, would produce something parochial, too closely linked with the needs of the manufacturing industries of the city.

In 1873 he published a pamphlet entitled *The Connection of the Universities and the Great Towns*. In those days the term 'Universities' meant Oxford and Cambridge even though the Scottish universities and Trinity College Dublin had been thriving for centuries. In England London had University College, the "godless institution in Gower Street", and King's College, which wasn't godless, and there was a range of colleges at Durham, Newcastle and Manchester. Percival's ideas drew on Matthew Arnold and Cardinal Newman for their inspiration. He wanted his college to produce an effect of 'liberal culture', to become an intellectual centre. He suggested that, if the provincial towns provided buildings and equipment, the universities, from their vast endowments, might provide chairs and the personnel to fill them.

His pamphlet met with a ready response from the Master of Balliol, Benjamin Jowett. Jowett had become Master in 1870 and although he had not yet acquired the formidable reputation he afterwards enjoyed, he had already dedicated himself to the production of a cultivated and responsible *élite,* as he put it, 'inoculating England with Balliol'. He was scholarly, courageous and intimidating. An Oxford student broadsheet of 1881 described him:

> 'First come I. My name is Jowett.
> There's no knowledge but I know it.
> I am the Master of this College
> What I don't know isn't knowledge.'

Josephine Butler spoke of his "wonderful reticence and refinement coupled with strenuous and swift decided action when needful". As Jowett himself put it, "Never retreat. Never explain. Get it done and let them howl".

Jowett brought these decisive qualities to Percival's scheme. He offered Bristol promises of sponsorship and financial help, not only from his own College but from New College, if the promoters would widen their Science scheme by including Literature and if they would admit women on a basis of equality with men.

A great meeting in the presence of the President of the British Association and Sir William Thompson (later Lord Kelvin) was held at the Victoria Rooms on 11 June 1874 "to promote a School of Science and Literature for the West of England". Percival and Jowett argued persuasively that Bristol needed the prestige of its own university, and that the development of modern urban life and work created a need for some form of outlet for the passions, enthusiasms and creativity unrelieved by the tedium of industrial routine. A university could create a means of organising the cultural pursuits of the people and it could produce physicians or engineers whose interests went beyond those needed solely for their profession.

The Victoria Rooms meeting was a partial success. The scheme to promote a School of Science and Literature for the West of England was successfully converted into a scheme to promote a University College for Bristol. The support of influential and affluent local families such as the Frys was gained. But there was one significant failure. The affluent members of Bristol society who were willing to give their goodwill and finance to the venture were largely Non-Conformists and Quakers in religion.

Christian action which manifested itself in promoting education was not the preserve of the Non-Conformists. All the major denominations shared the same sort of perceptions about what was needed, but the Non-Conformists' interests in social reform began to lead to a political involvement which in turn led them to challenge, as Liberals, the Anglican (and Tory) domination of the city and its institutions. The new University College became identified as a Non-Conformist and Liberal institution which attracted little Tory support. Indeed, the Tories, despite some initial grants to the new University College, soon began to develop, through the Society of Merchant Venturers, their own rival college. The consequent lack of

Bishop Percival. *Until 1897 he was also a member of the Firth College, Sheffield Council and was a founder member of the committee set up by the Government to administer grants to the English universities.*

Benjamin Jowett. *Bristol was fortunate to attract and retain the interest of this major figure in English nineteenth century life. His academic, and financial, support were crucial in the pre-Charter history of Bristol.*

3

finance, the lack of widespread community support and the existence of an academic rival inhibited the growth of the University College for almost all of its 33 years of existence.

But Jowett and Percival were determined to succeed, and in October 1876 the University College of Bristol opened its doors – rather modest ones in two houses in Park Row – to its first students. In keeping with Percival's ideas (and also to meet a stipulation in Jowett's offer of grants from Oxford) the new College was the first higher educational institution in England to admit women on a basis of equality with men.

The Principal of the new College was a friend of Percival's, Alfred Marshall. The 25-year-old Marshall had had to resign his Cambridge fellowship on the occasion of his marriage to Mary Paley, one of the first Newnham College *alumnae*. The quality of their relationship may be assessed by the fact that Mary Paley Marshall at their wedding promised to love and to honour her husband. The words, usual at the time, "to obey" were omitted. Marshall was already a distinguished economist when he came to Bristol, and his wife, also an academic, became the College's first lady lecturer.

The College opened with two professors and five lecturers. Later in the first term there were 11 lecturers. It offered courses in 15 subjects: Modern History, Modern Literature, Latin, Ancient History, French, German, Chemistry, Experimental Physics, Mathematics, Botany, Geology, Zoology, Political Economy and Law. In 1878 an Engineering course was added. The staff were young and included several such as Hele Shaw (Engineering), Silvanus Thompson (Physics), and Sollas (Geology), who achieved major national reputations in their disciplines. There was no particular curriculum and students could take whatever courses they liked. G. H. Leonard, for example, (later to become a Professor in the University) used the College to prepare for his Cambridge scholarship examination. Some of the women students who attended, as one of them put it, went there "to improve their after dinner conversation".

Initially, few courses were at a level that would be recognised today as 'higher education', but this has to be set against the generally poor provision of secondary education at the time (only Bristol Grammar School and Clifton College offered a reasonable standard of work in Bristol). By the 1880s, however, the College had produced its first graduates (London BAs for the most part).

Some courses were offered in remote locations such as Stroud, Bridgwater, Exeter and Cheltenham, and to meet the needs of students simple 'home study' kits were devised. Poverty was also the mother of one other innovation. The College offered evening classes in Bristol and part-time study – this led directly to the invention of the 'six month system', a

Blackboy Hill. *The City of Bristol was a very much smaller and quieter place when the University College was founded. Throughout its history, the University College never had more than a few hundred students in any one year.*

Park Row houses: *the first home of University College, Bristol.*

The original University College door: *now on a private house in Hotwells.*

Alfred Marshall. *The first Principal. Acknowledged by the famous J. M. Keynes as his master, Marshall was a founder of Economics as a discipline and a way of looking at the world. A pioneer of women's higher education in Bristol, he resisted it in later life at Cambridge.*

Sir William Ramsay. *The second Principal of University College, he was one of the eminent figures honoured by a 'Spy' cartoon. His discovery of neon and helium has affected everyone's life.*

Helium *filled air-ship over Fry's chocolate factory in Bristol.*

Neon signs.

combination of study and employment which is now called the 'sandwich' course.

The progress of the infant college was dogged by financial problems. Unlike Birmingham, Liverpool and other provincial colleges founded around the same time as Bristol, the University College failed to find its 'local Carnegie' – a local magnate who would solve all its financial problems at a stroke by erecting buildings, providing endowments and money for salaries sufficient to attract and hold good staff.

At the Victoria Rooms meeting it had been suggested that a capital sum of £25,000 and annual subscriptions for five years amounting to £3,000 would be sufficient. By July 1881 only £23,437 capital had been raised and the annual subscriptions fell short of what was required. In Liverpool over £80,000 was raised in two years, and even in Leeds, which considered itself poor, capital appeals had produced £110,000 by 1884. It was suggested that instead of the established motto "Knowledge is Power", it would be more appropriate for the University College of Bristol to have "College is Poor" as its watchword. (This sort of word-play delighted the Victorians. Professor Ryan, Professor of Engineering in the College, introduced the celebrated Clara Butt to her very first audience with the words "Here is Miss C. Butt, who is making her de-but".)

The College was poor. It had already spent most of what little it had. It had acquired a site beside the Rifle Drill Hall (near the City Museum and Art Gallery) facing the site for Bristol Grammar School's new buildings. The land had cost £3,250 and the first phase of an impressive college quadrangle by Charles Hansom, the brother of the man who invented the Hansom cab, had cost over £6,000. Most of the remaining capital had been absorbed by accumulated deficits. By 1881 Marshall felt he could go on no longer. He had been plagued with ill-health and the job of trying to build a new college left him little time for the reading and reflection necessary for his work. He also found the continual need to beg money distasteful. After being talked out of an attempt to leave in 1879, he told the College Council of his firm resolution to resign. He had been helped by the knowledge that the poverty of the College would not prevent it finding a suitable candidate for the principalship: the obvious successor was a newly appointed member of staff, the Professor of Chemistry, William Ramsay.

Ramsay was a 27-year-old Scot who had been educated at Glasgow and Tübingen Universities. His Scottish and German background influenced his view of what a university should be. In a lecture later in his life he set out his views. A university, he said, "is not merely a place where known facts and theories should be administered in daily doses to young men and women. The duty of the professors, assistant professors, teachers and advanced students is to increase knowledge". The German universities, he noted, possessed what they called a Philosophical Faculty which he translated as a

The Rifle Drill Hall. *A favourite venue for circuses and other entertainments.*

University College, Bristol.

Ryan's Christmas cards. *A lively sense of what was important, and funny, to Victorian Bristol.*

faculty which loves learning and wisdom. "The watchword of this faculty is Research; the searching out of the secrets of nature . . . the attempt to create new knowledge." The most important function of a university was to answer the question "why?". But in most cases, one had to be content with answering the question "how?". "The better we can learn *how* things are, the more nearly we will be able to say *why* they are." Everything in the University – the selection of teachers, the equipment of the laboratories and the libraries, and the awarding of degrees – must be devised to this end, and students must learn by trying to do something new, an idea that sat easily with Jowett's view that the true aim of the university teacher was to make students think for themselves.

For Ramsay in 1881, however, the central problem was finance. He was a man of great energy and flung himself into the task. He travelled widely and spoke to as many potential students as he could find. He embarked upon a round of dinner parties with the influential classes in Bristol. The College spent some of its small store of money on extending buildings (including a new, small but well-equipped laboratory for the Principal). But in May 1884 the Treasurer reported that by July all funds would be exhausted. The College scraped through 1885 but in 1886 matters were so serious that two professors were given notice of dismissal and it was announced that their departments were to be placed on a self-supporting basis.

Bristol was not the only new University College facing financial problems. In 1884 Ramsay went to Canada for a meeting of the British Association for the Advancement of Science. On his way home he discussed the problem of college financing with Veriamu Jones of Cardiff and W. M. Hicks, Principal of Firth College (later the University of) Sheffield. Cardiff, as a Welsh College, received Government support. The English colleges did not. Bristol and Sheffield agreed to call a meeting at Cambridge in January 1885 to discuss the problem with the other English colleges. A few months later the college principals met again in Birmingham and by April 1886 they had formed themselves into a committee to gain Government support in the form of grants. Jowett, Percival and other influential people lent their support and in February 1889 the Government announced that it had decided to recognise the English university colleges as national institutions by voting a grant of £15,000 a year. The mechanism by which the grants would be paid was determined by two Treasury Minutes of 11 March and 1 July 1889. These two Minutes created the nucleus of the present system of University finance: the Government was prepared to give financial aid but did not seek any form of control beyond establishing a form of review which could determine whether further support was needed. Bristol's share was £1,200.

In June 1887 Ramsay resigned on appointment to the Chair of Chemistry at University College, London. His successor was Conwy Lloyd Morgan, who, despite his name, was not a Welshman. He had been a professor at the

Veriamu Jones. *A brilliant Cambridge mathematician, he was appointed Principal of Firth College, Sheffield when he was 25 years old. He left just over a year later to become Principal of Cardiff in his native Wales.*

W. M. Hicks. *Veriamu Jones' successor at Sheffield, for over 20 years, as a close friend of Ramsay, he had an indirect but important influence on the fortunes of Bristol.*

University College, Bristol. *The last photograph of the academic staff taken in summer 1909. The ladies are: on the left Miss Pearce (Botany) and Miss Staveley (Women's Tutor).*

Early Days. *Laboratory staff and students in the Physics Laboratory around the turn of the century.*

University of Cape Town and came to Bristol first to teach Geology. He had studied under Huxley and at Bristol his broadening interest in philosophy and biology led him to study animal behaviour, and to become one of the first experimental psychologists. When Ramsay left, funds would not permit an attractive enough salary for the College Council to seek a successor in the Principalship. Lloyd Morgan was asked to succeed Ramsay and to accept a temporary appointment for 18 months with the title of Dean and Academical Head. The appointment was renewed annually until 1891 when he became Principal.

By that time, the College's financial problems had been alleviated although not removed. Lack of local support restricted the benefit Bristol could derive from the Government grant – the Treasury Minutes stipulated that "no grant to any College should exceed a quarter of its income, local income from fees, endowments and subscriptions". But another Government Act provided unexpected help. The Technical Instruction Act empowered local authorities to levy a rate for technical instruction. In 1890 the local Technical Instruction Committees received unforeseen revenue in the form of "whisky money", sums initially set aside to compensate publicans who lost their licences and which the Government applied to technical instruction. The Bristol Committee voted £2,000 to the College and gave it a further £500 grant in return for some free places for students.

Warring institutions. *The Bristol Royal Infirmary and the Bristol General Hospital.*

The College spent the new money on a much needed Engineering Block which began the third side of Hansom's quadrangle. The Engineering Block, which released much needed space to Physics, was completed in October 1893. Just a few months earlier the College completed another significant development – a building (designed by F. Bligh Bond) to house the Medical School which was formally incorporated into the College in April 1893.

The Bristol Medical School had started in 1833 to provide a systematic instruction for the students who 'walked the wards' in the Infirmary (founded in 1737), the Clifton Dispensary (founded in 1812) and the General Hospital (founded in 1832). In 1873, its poverty and poor buildings led it to seek an association with the Bristol Museum and Library which had been formed in 1867 through the amalgamation of the Bristol Library Society (1772) and the Bristol Institution for the Advancement of Science, Literature and the Arts (*c.* 1805). The Museum and Library were the promoters of the scheme for a College of Science, the scheme which Percival and Jowett had translated into the University College. In the 1870s the Medical School was split on polictical lines (the Infirmary was Tory; the General Hospital was Liberal) and for some years political problems damaged the development of the School and its previously high academic reputation. But an agreement of affiliation to the University College was secured in 1879 and the Faculty which formally joined the College in 1893 was united and had restored its academic reputation.

Lunsford House. *Reputed to be the first home of the Bristol Medical School. Certainly anatomy was taught in adjacent buildings, demolished to provide a site for the present School of Chemistry.*

Other subjects were also making pleasing progress. Sydney Young in Chemistry, Chattock (Physics), Stanton and Ferrier (Engineering) had established national reputations. The Engineering course at Bristol still had few rivals in offering "the six month system" in which students spent six months in industry and six months in the College. Students from the three Day Training Colleges for teachers – Women's College (1892), Men's College (1905) and Secondary Training Department (1902) – attended College lectures. The College had at least the nucleus of all the departments which characterise the University today.

In 1896 the commissioners appointed by the Treasury for grant purposes reported, "On the Science side generally as on the Arts side, there is evidently vigorous life in the place, and the work done is of the University type". In 1902 they reported, "Solid educational work is being done . . . The College has done much . . . to encourage research and postgraduate work. It suffers, however, from want of money".

In the years since 1876 the College had achieved much. It had a small stock of useful, well-equipped buildings. Its first three Principals had been outstanding men, probably the major scholars of their time in their own disciplines. The academic standards of the students were rising all the time. The experiment of educating women had already brought, from among the first women students, the first women members of staff in Mary Fry (Mrs Napier Abbott) and Marion Pease, Mistress of Method in the Day Training College.

But other university colleges elsewhere, more fortunately provided, were obtaining charters and becoming universities in their own right. In 1902 Birmingham received its Royal Charter, in 1903 Liverpool, in 1904 Leeds, and in 1905, Sheffield. If Bristol were to follow in their footsteps, the College would need a new initiative, a force that would break the stalemate between Tory and Liberal, Anglican and Non-Conformist, and procure the support of a major philanthropist. As the College entered the new century there seemed little sign that Bristol itself could produce such a force. At this point, Ramsay made another crucial intervention in Bristol's affairs. When the Chair of Chemistry fell vacant, he recommended to the College Council that they should appoint his young assistant, Morris Travers.

Chapter Two

The Charter Campaign

It would be wrong to suggest that no steps towards translating the University College, Bristol into a full university with its own Charter had been taken before Morris Travers succeeded Sydney Young as Professor of Chemistry in 1904. Lewis Fry, J. W. Arrowsmith and others on the Council were fully aware of the need to progress and to attract more financial support. At times, had it not been for donations given anonymously by Mr Fenwick Richards, the College would have collapsed. Fry and Arrowsmith were also fully aware that broader local support was needed. The College's problem was that it was regarded as a Liberal foundation, and this was reflected in its funding. The Anchor Society (one of the three societies founded in memory of the educational philanthropist Edward Colston (1636–1721)) was Liberal politically and contributed to the College. The predominantly Tory Dolphin Society did not. Arrowsmith and Walter Reid, proprietor of the *Western Daily Press,* decided to initiate a new Colston Society which would be non-political and which could draw adherents of both parties into supporting the University College. They founded the University College Colston Society. They hoped only for some increase in support for research, but their new Society had a central role in the founding of the University.

In late Victorian times such societies did much of their work by holding dinners at which speeches were made and funds were solicited and collected. At the first Colston Society dinner held on 7 December 1899 (significantly, it was chaired by Percival, who was by then Bishop of Hereford) the guest speaker was James (later Viscount) Bryce. Bryce spoke of the possibility that Bristol might some day be the home of a western university. At that time there was a great debate whether a university should be an examining university (one which prepared and supervised the examination of students who were taught by a wide range of other colleges) or an autonomous teaching university, (one which taught *and* examined its own students). Bryce was firmly against what he called "Lilliputian universities" which gave their own degrees. His views were widely shared. Mowat, Permanent Secretary of the Treasury, for example, said, "The multiplication of degree-

Morris Travers. *Pictured about the time he joined the University College, Bristol.*

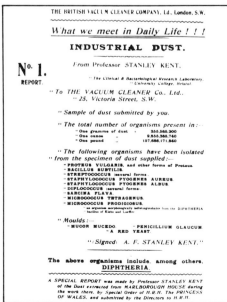

The first vacuum cleaner. *An early example of Bristol research helping industry.*

giving bodies in a state is the certain forerunner of a depreciation in the value of a degree". As Lord Ashby points out, the observation 'more means worse', much canvassed in the late 1960s and 1970s, is not an original observation.

In 1900 a committee was set up under the chairmanship of the Bishop of Bristol with A. F. Stanley Kent, Professor of Physiology, as Secretary, who had suggested that the College Senate should examine the practicalities of a university for the west. But at the first meeting of the committee when it was agreed that the first practical step that needed to be taken to found such a university, an examining university, would be the appointment of a Registrar, the Bishop of Bristol sadly pointed out that to get the right person a salary of £1,000 a year would be required. No one could think how such a sum, and the endowment it implied, could be raised. The committee adjourned and never had another meeting.

In 1901, at an annual general meeting of the College, Percival returned to the idea of an autonomous university when he spoke of a Bristol and West of England University. But a year later, at the third Colston dinner R. B. (later Lord) Haldane envisaged a federal West of England University of which University College, Bristol, the Merchant Venturers' Technical College, Bristol and the colleges at Reading, Southampton and Exeter might form the constituents. Haldane was a known proponent of autonomous universities but even this concession to the federal idea failed to provoke any sign of support.

It was into this situation of earnest desire, low income and failing hope that Morris Travers arrived. Travers had worked with Ramsay at University College, London, on the discovery of rare gases and came to Bristol at the age of 32 with a well-established scientific reputation. He was elected a Fellow of the Royal Society just after he took up his post. In Bristol he quickly established a reputation for bluntness in speech and decisiveness in action. A. M. Tyndall towards the end of his long life reported a conversation which he said was typical of Travers.

"What are your plans for a university?", said Travers immediately on arrival at Bristol.

"Oh well, you know we haven't got any money yet." (The Government of the day had recently laid it down that a college needed at least £100,000 in endowments before it could apply for a Charter.)

"I said, what are your plans?"

"Well, you know it's no good making plans until you know how much money you're going to get."

"Stuff and nonsense, I've never heard such rubbish." (Tyndall said Travers was quite capable of speaking thus to a man he had just met for the first time.) "You'll never get any money until you make some plans."

To Tyndall and others who were on the staff at the time it seemed that Travers said such things entirely as his own idea. But Ramsay's letters reveal that early in 1904 he was writing to Travers in Bristol advising him not to have anything to do with the federal West of England University idea. "Stick out for your own university. Don't yield to Southampton's request for an Examining Board", he said. Since at that time Travers had not seen the Bishop of Bristol's report and had not heard of Haldane's 1902 speech it would seem that he and Ramsay were discussing Bristol in terms of London University where the teaching *v.* examining university controversy had raged during Travers' time at UCL.

Travers was already writing draft statutes based on the Birmingham model and was beginning to seek support politically and financially. In February 1904 Lady Ramsay, recalling her husband's methods in Bristol, wrote to Travers urging him to call on Mrs Albert Fry. Later she recommended that he call on Mrs Tribe "who might be able to interest her relatives, the Wills, in the scheme". In July 1904 Ramsay wrote again offering further advice on the draft constitution and in January 1905 he arranged for Travers to see R. B. Haldane about Government support for a Charter for Bristol.

R. B. Haldane.

Haldane was a Scot, from a class of Scottish society which traditionally sent their sons to Oxford or Cambridge, but he was educated at Edinburgh and Göttingen University in Germany. The contrast between his own university education and the university education then available in England made him ambitious to establish in England universities centred in the industrial cities, each, as in Germany, permeating the civil and industrial life of its region. As he said himself, he "lived for universities". Yet he never held any office connected with education in Government. At the age of 40 he had already played a leading role in the University of London Bill (1897) and he had been involved in gaining a charter for Birmingham. He had also been involved in a campaign with Ramsay and others – Lord Ashby suggests, "it was better described as a conspiracy" – to create in Imperial College an institution similar to the great polytechnic at Charlottenburg in Berlin. The proposed provincial universities were to be 'provincial Charlottenburgs'.

Haldane's view of the future of university education was plain. In October 1901 he had told a Liverpool audience, "The days of federated universities are over". His objections to federalism were equally clear. A federal university, he said, deprived professors of the *Lehrfreiheit* essential to their vocation; they were compelled to teach to a syllabus prescribed by a remote and impersonal examining body. Secondly, local citizens would not regard the local college as their college: it would only be an intellectual colony owing allegiance to a distant mother university.

When Liverpool University College petitioned the Privy Council to be allowed to secede from the federal Victoria University, the petition was

The Blind Asylum.

The Bristol Trade and Mining School in Nelson Street. *The building was originally used as a Diocesan School (1812-1852) but in 1856, partly as the result of the Great Exhibition of 1851, it became the Bristol Diocesan Trade and Mining School with classes for adults in Chemistry, Mining and Engineering and offering instruction to young people in "the scientific principles upon which trades and manufactures are based". It was the first of its kind in Britain. In 1863 it also became the home of the Society of Merchant Venturers' Navigation School which had started in 1595. In 1880 the Society bought premises in Unity Street. In 1885, with the agreement of the Colston Trust, the Society took over the Trade School, changing its name to the 'Merchant Venturers' School' and endowing it with a new building designed by E. C. Robins.*

opposed by Yorkshire College at Leeds. The matter quickly ceased to be a squabble between two colleges and the issue to be decided went beyond the integrity of Victoria University. It became a debate about what sort of university education should be provided in England. Haldane persuaded the Government not to set up a Royal Commission but to decide the matter in Privy Council. On 7 December 1902 the Privy Council decided in Liverpool's favour in the particular issue: in the important national issue, Haldane's ideas of a network of autonomous provincial universities had been accepted and a number of other university colleges were quickly able to follow Liverpool's example in becoming autonomous.

When Travers put the idea of a University of Bristol to Haldane, therefore, he met with a warm response. Haldane gave him a copy of his 1902 speech at the Colston Society. The fact that no one in Bristol had drawn it to Travers' attention before then is an indication of how low-spirited the university movement in Bristol had become. Haldane made it clear that as far as the Government was concerned there was no major objection in principle to be overcome. University College, Bristol needed only to obtain more local support and much more endowment money to be able to petition successfully for a Charter as the University of Bristol.

At this juncture even Travers' considerable nerve was stretched. In speaking to Haldane he had gone further than any sensible member of staff acting as an individual should have gone. He decided to go to see Lewis Fry, the Chairman of the College Council and confess all. They met on 1 February 1905. Fry was a member of the great Bristol Quaker family. He had retired from the House of Commons in 1900 when he was 68 and had been honoured by nomination as a Privy Councillor. He had been a founder of the College and had sustained it financially in its darkest days. He had succeeded his brother Albert as Chairman of the University College Council when he died in March 1903. Now, less than two years later, he faced Travers.

"Well, Professor Travers", he said. "We can dismiss you. Or we can proceed." Fry was more aware than Travers of the difficulties but he had no hesitation. "We will proceed." In Travers' view, the inception of the University dated from that moment. Bringing about the Charter took somewhat longer.

Fry set about mobilising support. His sister Mary Fry (Mrs Napier Abbott) wrote to the Duchess of Beaufort soliciting the Duke's goodwill. Lewis Fry himself found a key convert in Dr Ernest (later Sir Ernest) Cook, the Tory Chairman of the City Education Committee. With Fry and Cook's encouragement, Travers wrote a pamphlet setting out the case for the University. Goodenough Taylor, the editor of the Tory *Bristol Times and Mirror,* agreed to write editorials advocating public support for the scheme set out in articles by Travers which he would publish. Ferrier agreed to write

Lewis Fry: *in Travers' view, "the father of the University".*

The Great Fire at Merchant Venturers College.   Oct. 9th., 1906.

The Merchant Venturers' Technical College fire. *The damage was extensive but the College was soon rebuilt.*

Goldney. *The home of Lewis Fry, shown in Waterhouse's drawing of his remodelling of the original eighteenth century house. It was here that the early meetings of the University Committee and the informal meetings regarding the Charter took place.*

similar pieces for the Liberal *Western Daily Press*. By October 1905 Arrowsmith, who had previously been critical of Travers, saw a typewritten copy of the pamphlet and was converted. He published the pamphlet and soon after Travers was able to tell Fry that Haldane had confirmed that "the Government wanted to see a University established in Bristol". Travers travelled to Sheffield to see Hicks, Ramsay's friend and the new University of Sheffield's first Vice-Chancellor, who gave him valuable advice. He also made contact with prominent politicians like Walter Long and Sir Michael Hicks Beach. Everywhere he met encouragement.

Between September 1905 and January 1906 Travers must have felt that even Divine Providence smiled upon his project. On 26 September 1905 he noted that the Blind Asylum in Queen's Road at the top of Park Street would make a suitable site for his new University. Less than a month later he picked up a telephone on a line shared with the Asylum and overheard a conversation which revealed that the Trustees of the Asylum were preparing to sell the building. He informed Fry and suggested the College buy the building at once. Although there were problems about raising the necessary money, Fry again decided to back Travers and the Blind Asylum was bought with the aid of J. S. Fry and some members of the Wills family.

In January 1906 there was another fortunate occurrence for the University campaign. The Merchant Venturers' Technical College was destroyed by fire. This immediately faced the Merchant Venturers with a problem about the future of their College which they had deliberately built as a rival to the University College. When, shortly after the University College was founded, the Merchant Venturers perceived that it appeared to be dominated by Liberals, they had set about developing the Bristol Trade School which they had taken over in 1875. With the able academic leadership of Julius Wertheimer, they had created a College which taught a wide range of subjects for the London University degree. Students of the College obtained excellent results and by 1905 the Merchant Venturers' College had become a very well-established and rival focus of higher education with its own excellent buildings in Unity Street. The January 1906 fire did not bring the College to an end but it provided sufficient opportunity for Dr Cook to have a series of meetings with the Master of the Merchant Venturers about its future and the proposed University. Despite Wertheimer's objections, a measure of agreement was reached and by July 1906 Cook was able to report informally that the Merchant Venturers were no longer opposed to the University scheme.

By then matters had advanced so far that Lewis Fry felt it was time to put the scheme to promote a University for Bristol on a formal basis. On 6 March he convened a meeting preliminary to the establishment of a University Committee. He was able to announce that £30,000 to form the nucleus of the necessary endowment fund had been given by Lord

Julius Wertheimer. He succeeded Thomas Coomber as Headmaster of the Merchant Venturers' School in 1890 and became first Principal of the Merchant Venturers' Technical College when it was formed in 1894. He, G. H. Pope and W. W. Ward, were responsible for the Society of Merchant Venturers' side of the negotiations with the University College about a Charter. Born in Birmingham, he was educated at University College, Liverpool and Owen's College, Manchester. He was Head of Leeds' College of Science and Technology. He took the first X-ray photographs in Bristol and the first surgical operation in Bristol in which X-rays were used was performed on the basis of X-ray photographs taken by him. He saw the role of his College largely in terms of teaching and was critical of Professor Ferrier who, he noted scornfully, did only 12 hours of teaching a week because of his research commitments. In their multi-level of approach to disciplines and their heavy emphasis on teaching rather than research-with-teaching, Wertheimer's ideas on higher education foreshadow the theory of the present polytechnics.

Inset at top: HENRY OVERTON WILLS.
Standing, left to right: J. RAFTER, R. P. COWL, J. H. HOWELL, E. H. COOK, H. N. ABBOT, C. LLOYD MORGAN.
Sitting, left to right: HIATT C. BAKER, F. RICHARDSON CROSS, G. A. WILLS, LEWIS FRY, J. W. ARROWSMITH, FENWICK RICHARDS, C. J. LOVE.
In front: T. W. WILLIAMS.

Committee appointed for obtaining Charter for University of Bristol

The University Committee.

Winterstoke (a member of the Wills family), Sir Frederick Wills, J. S. Fry and F. J. Fry. On 2 July 1906, a widely based committee of about 100 persons was formed. An executive committee with Travers as Secretary was elected. The Committee, partly due to Haldane's advice, had a large number of Tories.

Negotiations with the Society of Merchant Venturers continued on a more formal basis. In December 1906 the Merchants suggested that their college might become part of the University as its Faculty of Applied Science with a substantial degree of financial autonomy although subject to the University with regard to curriculum and academic matters. This was a little too close to the federal idea of a University and Fry replied, on behalf of his Committee, that they wanted "complete fusion and amalgamation" of the departments of the two institutions and that there should be "one administration, financial and educational" on which the Society would be represented. The Merchant Venturers felt unable to agree to this and in March 1907 negotiations were broken off. The Unity Street buildings were restored as those of an independent college.

The Committee also had another setback. Since 1900 Ramsay had been negotiating with prominent people in India concerning the foundation of an Indian Research Institution. By 1906 the idea had come to fruition and Travers was appointed to be its first Director. So Travers left the work of

PUT A PENNY IN THE SLOT.
Dr. Cook (to Young Bristol): "It's all right, my little man; you'll get value for your money by-and-bye."

founding one university to direct the founding of another, the Indian Research Institute at Bangalore. He was not completely sorry to leave Bristol. The energy with which he had pursued his scheme for the University and the independent line he frequently followed had not made everyone his friend. There were those who spoke disparagingly of the scheme to found 'Travers' University'. Travers handed over the secretaryship of the University Committee to Richard Cowl, the Professor of English in the University College with whom he had developed a close working relationship. Travers had been in Bristol only three and three-quarter years. When he came a University for Bristol had seemed an impossible dream. When he was in Bristol, he had been, as Tyndall put it, "a breath of fresh air". When he left, the dream was half-way to reality.

But real problems remained. The chief one was financial. By January 1908 the endowments promised for the University still stood at £30,000, the total announced by Fry nearly two years before and originally contributed to buy the Blind Asylum. It seemed as if all the Committee's strenuous efforts might still come to nothing. The situation was transformed when George Wills, President of the Colston Research Society, received a note from his father H. O. Wills. At the ninth Colston dinner in 1908, George Wills read it to the assembled company: "I have decided to promise One hundred thousand pounds towards the Endowment of a University for Bristol & the West of England, provided a Charter be granted within two years from this date . . . Please announce this at your Dinner tomorrow, and say that I trust that this help may fairly launch our University at no distant date."

Tyndall, who was there, recalled "The atmosphere on the announcement of this gift of what seemed a complete fortune was electric. We all stood up, waved our napkins and proceeded *recklessly* to order champagne at 7/6 a bottle". There was more good news. J. W. Arrowsmith announced that four

How Bristol saw the Charter campaign. The local newsapers had great fun with the campaigners. The first cartoon shows Dr Cook persuading Bristol to pay a penny rate in support of the University. City support, although reduced to a nominal amount in later years, continued until the 1970s. In the second, J. W. Arrowsmith plots with an appropriately dressed Napier Abbott, Wills' family solicitor, as H. O. Wills approaches on horseback bearing a bag of gold. Haldane and Augustine Birrell, the President of the Board of Education (the equivalent of today's Secretary of State for Education and Science), look on. Birrell was a Bristol MP.

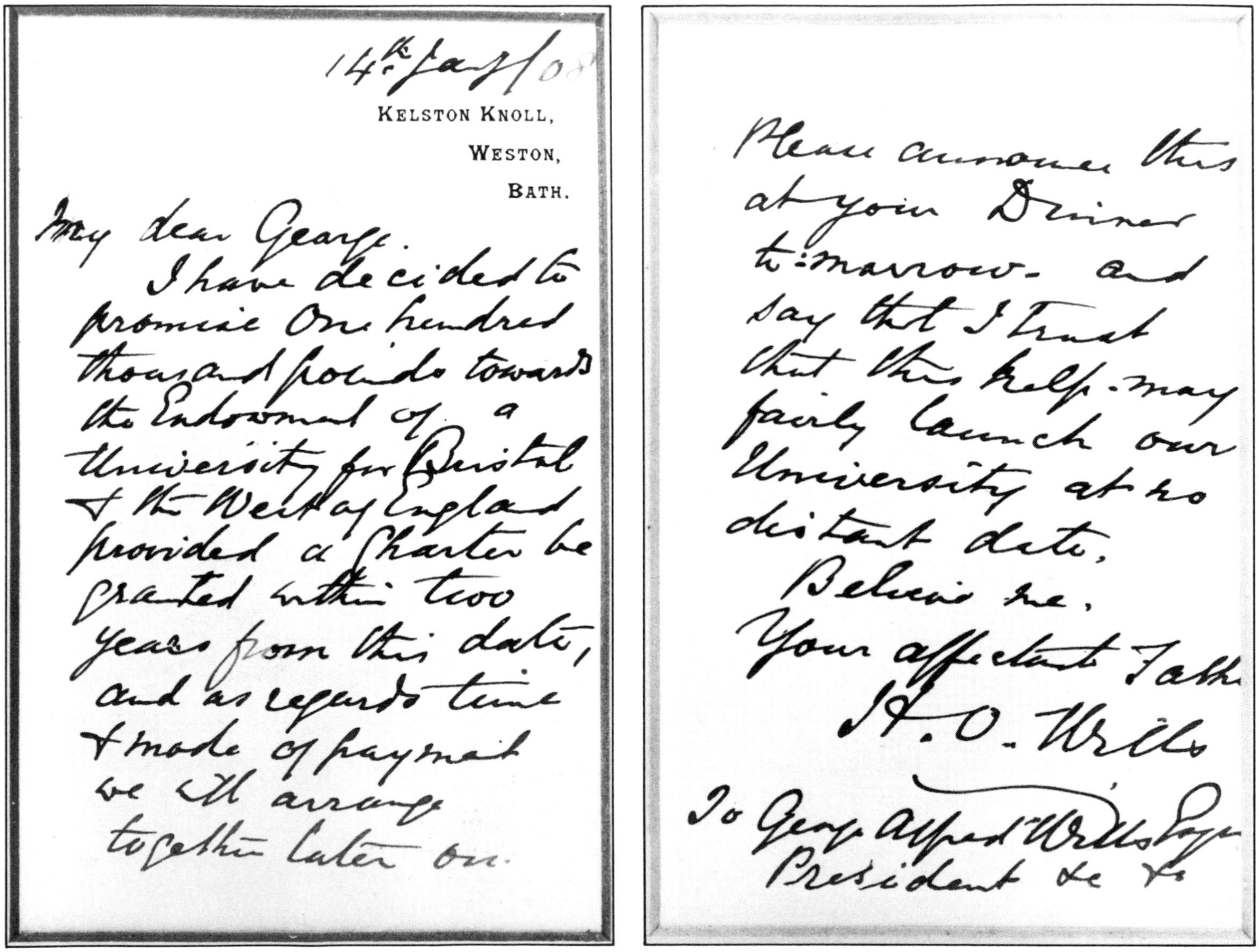

14ᵗʰ Jany/08

KELSTON KNOLL,

WESTON,

BATH.

My dear George.

I have decided to promise One hundred thousand pounds towards the Endowment of a University for Bristol & the West of England provided a Charter be granted within two years from this date, and as regards time & mode of payment we will arrange together later on.

Please announce this at your Dinner to-morrow. and say that I trust that this help. may fairly launch our University at no distant date,

Believe me,

Your affectionate Father

H. O. Wills

To George Alfred Wills Esqr
President &c &c

H. O. Wills' note *announcing his gift. The Wills family were succinct when offering their enormous benefactions.*

The Rival College. *The Merchant Venturers' Technical College.*

offers of £1,000 and a promise of £10,000 had been made during the dinner. A note was then sent up by P. J. Worsley to say that he would be pleased to give £2,000. The day ended with the endowment fund standing at five times what it had started at that morning – in 24 hours the University scheme had attracted more funds than the College had acquired throughout its entire history.

The University Committee set to work with renewed vigour. Negotiations with the Merchant Venturers were resumed. Agreement was eventually reached. The two Engineering Departments were to be united to form the new Faculty of Engineering, all Engineering teaching was to be done at Unity Street. Wertheimer was to be permanent Dean with his own Department of Chemical Engineering and the MVTC's non-Engineering teaching, which included subjects like photography, dressmaking and plumbing as well as theoretical sciences, was to develop separately educationally and financially. Over 50 years later and as a result of some quite different local and national events some of these remaining departments were translated to the neighbouring city of Bath to form a new University of Technology. Others became the nucleus of Bristol Polytechnic.

Further financial help was offered. As a result of the influence of Dr Cook and some judicious prompting from the Government arranged by Arrowsmith through Haldane the City Council offered the proceeds of a penny rate (about £7,000 per annum) if the Charter could be obtained. The endowment fund continued to grow and soon exceeded £200,000. Since grants from the Government were linked to endowments, this enormous endowment carried with it implications of future increased Government funding. From being one of the poorest colleges, Bristol had suddenly become one of the richest.

Public support continued to grow. On the occasion of a Royal visit in July 1908, a Loyal Address was presented to King Edward VII by Percival, Fry and Lloyd Morgan. Two petitions seeking a Charter were presented to the Privy Council. One represented the views of the University Committee, the other an alternative by Wertheimer seeking a larger measure of independence for the Merchant Venturers' College departments. The Committee's view easily prevailed and on the afternoon of 17 May 1909 news was received that the King in Privy Council had assented to the creation of the University of Bristol. Flags were flown from the Council House, the Exchange and many other public buildings in the city. The bells of the city's churches rang out. The Sign Manual was attached to the Charter on 24 May. The dream that had begun at the Victoria Rooms meeting 35 years earlier had become a reality in institutional terms. It now remained to be seen whether the new University could also fulfil the academic dreams of Percival, Jowett, Ramsay and the others who had influenced the College.

Success at last: *a note received by Travers in India.*

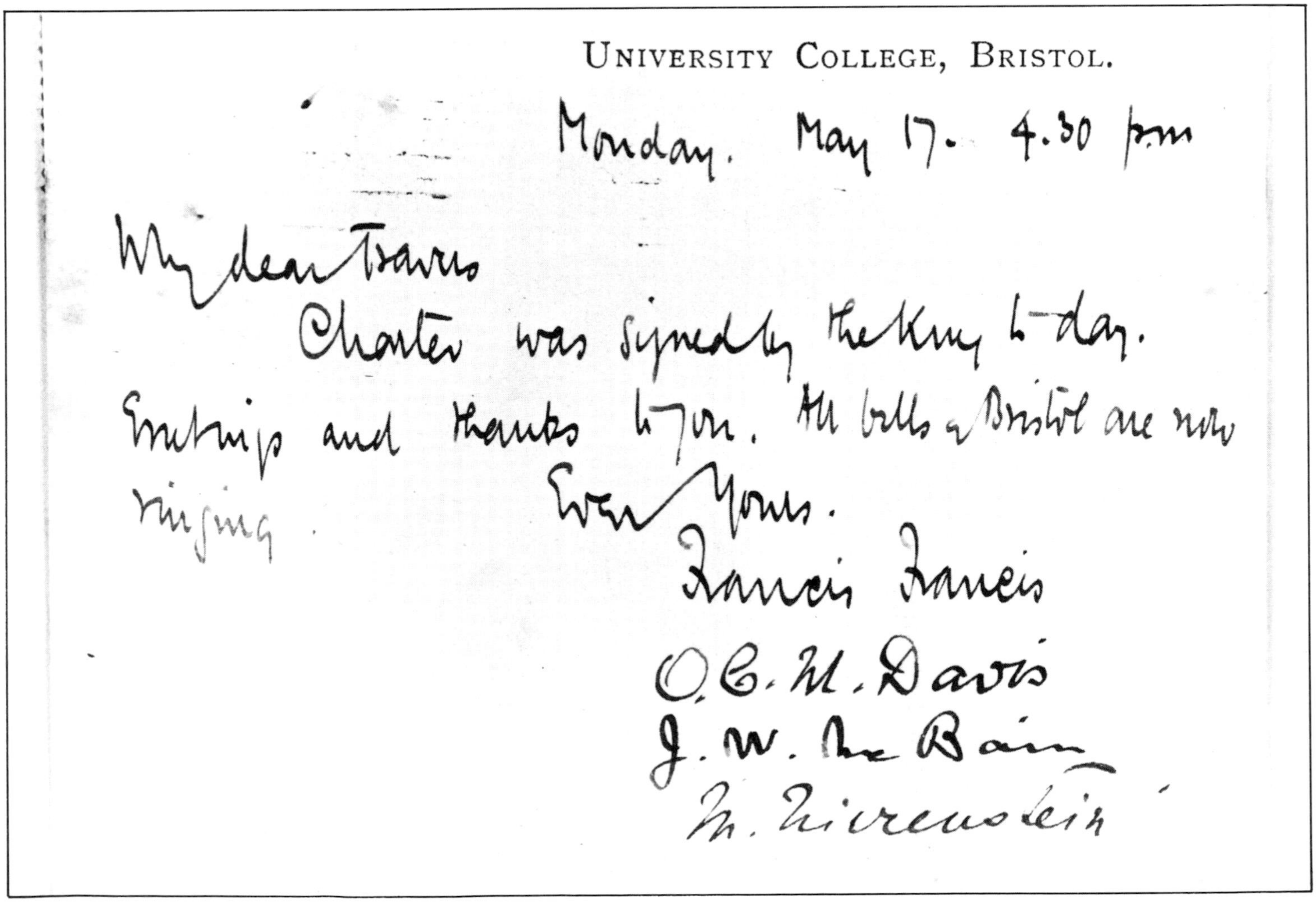

UNIVERSITY COLLEGE, BRISTOL.

Monday. May 17. 4.30 pm

My dear Travers

Charter was signed by the King to-day. Greetings and thanks to you. All bells of Bristol are now ringing.

Ever Yours.

Francis Francis

O. C. M. Davis

J. W. McBain

M. Nierenstein

Chapter Three

Building a University

The Charter which Bristol received was typical of the Charters granted to the new universities made independent in the first decade of the new century. Previous universities had been for the most part federations of colleges which taught for examinations set by the University and not by college lecturers. The new universities were unified and autonomous; the degrees were, so to speak, certificates awarded by the professors who taught the students. The university colleges which preceded the new universities had usually decided all matters – financial, executive and academic – in their Councils, bodies with a very large lay membership with only minimal representation of the teaching staff and none at all of the students. The new Charters set up a system which comprised a widely representative body, the Court, which was to meet usually about once a year – this was broadly equivalent to the Annual General Meeting which the university colleges had had to hold because legally they were limited companies. The financial and executive powers of the University were vested in the Council, a body which continued to have a predominance of lay members but which now included a larger percentage of academics. The Senate, which consisted of the Professors of the University, was given the power of regulating the academic affairs. Finally, the Charter provided for a Guild of Undergraduates which would represent the students and serve as an electoral college to produce a few student members of Court.

These ideas seem commonplace today, but in the first decade of the century the benefits of such ideas were by no means manifest or accepted by all. In Bristol, for example, Arrowsmith cheerfully told Travers with whom he was playing golf, "The academic staff are there to do what they are told", and Ryan, the Professor of Engineering, had to threaten to resign in order to get time to do research. Where did these ideas come from?

The Scottish influence is again apparent. The first of the new universities was Birmingham which was created out of Mason's College. The prime mover in obtaining Birmingham's Charter was Joseph Chamberlain. Chamberlain himself had not been to university but in 1858 students in Scotland had been given the right to elect a Rector who would serve as their

J. M. Mackay and disciples at Liverpool.

representative. In 1897 Chamberlain was elected Rector of Glasgow. He was greatly impressed by what he saw there. As he left Glasgow he remarked, "When I go back to Birmingham, I mean to have a university of my own". If the matter had been left simply to Chamberlain, Birmingham University might have perpetuated lay control through its Council. But the Constitution of Birmingham was influenced crucially by others. Mason's College professors, led by E. A. Sonnenschein, the Professor of Classics, produced their own draft of the Constitution which established a 'faculty-run' University with a strong Senate.

The inspiration behind Sonnenschein's campaign came from another Scot, the Rathbone Professor of History at Liverpool, J. M. Mackay. In the opinion of Lord Ashby, "Mackay's monument is the style of government in the civic universities of England . . . Mackay's mission, which he pursued with the forceful, and often tiresome, persistence of a zealot, was to ensure that academic affairs were controlled by academics. He did not invent the familiar two-tier system of government in the English civic universities (that was the work of another Scot, James Bryce); but it was Mackay whose compelling advocacy helped to define the balance of power between these two tiers: an unequivocal delegation of academic decisions to faculties under democratically elected deans".

But though the broad framework of the Charter which Bristol received reflected the influence of Birmingham's Charter and therefore of Scots, the detail – the Statutes, Ordinances and Regulations – was, according to Tyndall, the work of a Welshman, Sir Isambard Owen. As early as 1906 Conwy Lloyd Morgan indicated that he wanted to give up the Principalship of the University College. When the Charter was granted he consented to become the first Vice-Chancellor but, like Hicks of Sheffield in similar circumstances, with the firm stipulation that he would hand over the post after a very short period. The increase in Bristol endowments was too recent to allow the Council to believe that it could attract a prestigious academic candidate for the post from Oxford or Cambridge. The difficult negotiations with the Merchant Venturers were also too recent to allow much hope that

H. O. Wills: *the University of Bristol's first Chancellor in full regalia.*

the creation of the new University would be a simple task. Apart from the presence of strongly flavoured characters like Wertheimer, with whom the Merchant Venturers' College had endowed the new University, the Council was also aware that the quality of staff the University would inherit from the University College was uneven. In these circumstances they turned to a Welshman, skilled and experienced in academic diplomacy, Sir Isambard Owen.

Owen had already shown his capacities in dealing with intractable problems in the University of Wales and at King's College, Newcastle. The godson of Isambard Kingdom Brunel and the son of Brunel's deputy engineer, he proved to be an admirable choice for Bristol and busied himself with all sorts of matters, even designing the colours of the gowns and hoods for the graduates. (Tyndall found the clash of pink and red disturbing but added that Owen was trying to replicate the colour of the rocks in the Avon Gorge after rain.)

Some of the difficulties anticipated by the Council materialised. It was decided that three of the College 'Chairs' should be re-advertised and the occupants invited to apply. Only Cowl, who had succeeded Travers as Secretary of the University Committee, was not reappointed. He was offered a Fellowship which he held for about a year before resigning, his academic career in irretrievable ruin. The ill-feeling created by Cowl's treatment produced a climate of discontent in which personal feelings of a rancorous kind ran deep. There were threats of writs for defamation. Unfortunately, through the best of motives, the new University gave the malcontents an opportunity for public criticism.

According to Tyndall, Cowl's treatment provoked the premature resignation of A. P. Chattock from the Chair of Physics. Despite his great reputation Chattock curiously had no first degree and he felt that if Cowl's suitability for a Chair was called in question then his own ability to confer degrees upon students was in doubt. Chattock made useful contributions in a number of disciplines. Before he joined University College he had been responsible for devising the lights on the fairies in the very first production of Gilbert and Sullivan's *Iolanthe*. The wind gauge which he devised was a standard instrument used in wind tunnels for very many years and Sir Oliver Lodge recalled that had he taken Chattock's advice he might have discovered air waves before Hertz. After his retirement Chattock devoted his time to studying animal behaviour, particularly chickens. He produced a number of papers in this area particularly one with Grindley on the memory of chickens, before returning for a few years to make some more contributions to physics in his old age.

When the Charter was granted H. O. Wills became the first Chancellor, and when he died the University invited Haldane to succeed him. The occasion of Haldane's installation was seen as an opportunity to thank and to

The new University Council.

honour all those who had sustained the University College through its darkest days and who had supported the campaign for the Charter. It was agreed to offer 70 Honorary Degrees. This in itself was not an improper procedure. As Tyndall pointed out many years later, Glasgow celebrated its quincentenary with the award of about 50 Honorary Degrees. But in 1912 for a University, itself not three years old and which was one of a group of new universities founded in controversial circumstances within the previous ten years, to propose so many degrees was ill-advised. It seemed to confirm the view of Bryce and others that 'more means worse'. The situation was exacerbated by an article in *The Observer* which made a violent attack upon the lay members of the University. The storm grew and the representative of the University of Oxford on the Court caused a special meeting of that body to be called to debate a motion which asked that the Visitor (in effect the Privy Council) should be called upon to make an investigation into the affairs of the University of Bristol. But the City and the University united under this threat and the resolution was defeated at Court by around 200 votes to 3. The agitation died slowly but, as Tyndall recalled, "there was a smear on our good name for many years".

The installation ceremony at which the controversial Honorary Degrees were conferred had been made necessary by the demise of H. O. Wills; but the single most important factor in removing the 'smear' was occasioned by the memorial of the first Chancellor. His sons, George and Harry Wills, decided to give the University a new main building on the Blind Asylum site as a memorial building to their father. Everything had to be of the best, regardless of expense. As Tyndall pointed out, "At that time it must have meant that they were prepared to give at least two or three hundred thousand pounds and it was far more than that in the end". Their idea was merely to do something for the city of Bristol but, psychologically, thinking people said to themselves, "Look here, Bristol University can't be such a rotten place if hard-headed businessmen are prepared to put down hundreds of thousands of pounds in its support". A gift of this magnitude to a new university was unprecedented, but the offer to fund a new main building was not the end of

George Wills.

Harry Wills.

29

Making a University: *the money which backed the Wills family munificence was created by the tobacco workers of the Bedminster factory.*

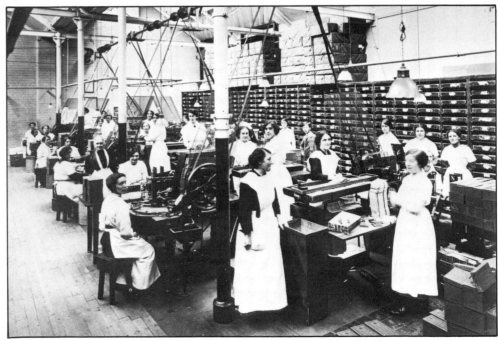

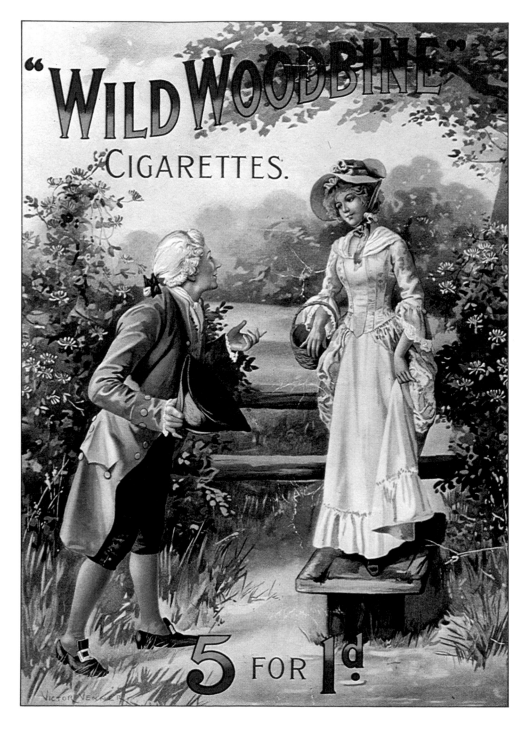

Woodbine. *The cornerstone of the Wills tobacco empire was the popular Woodbine cigarette. The Victorian and Edwardian public could also recognise the wild flower which gave it its name in the advertising of the day. The charming picture is by Victor Venner 1905.*

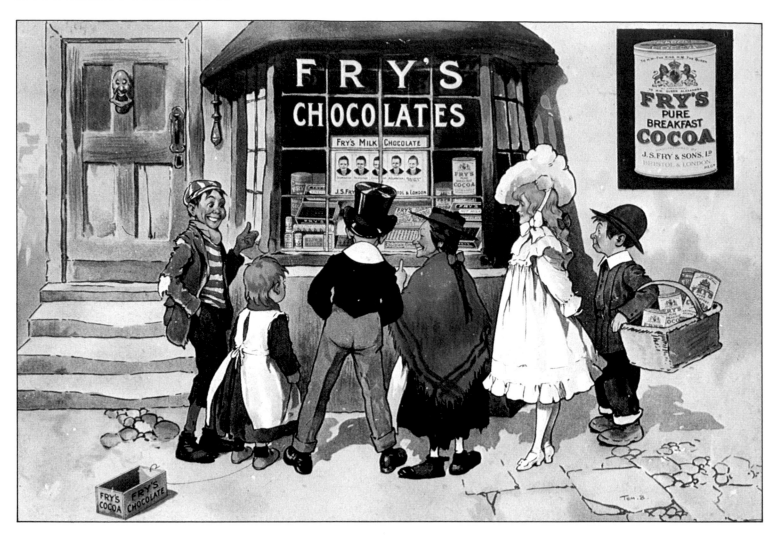

Fry's Chocolate. *The workers at Fry's (then in central Bristol) made their contribution too to the private fortunes which were used to support the University College and the University.*

The most famous names of Fry's products, such as "Five Boys", are now seen with increasing rarity. The company is now part of Cadbury-Schweppes, and the new owners (since 1934) do not see the Fry's name as a useful part of their current marketing strategy.

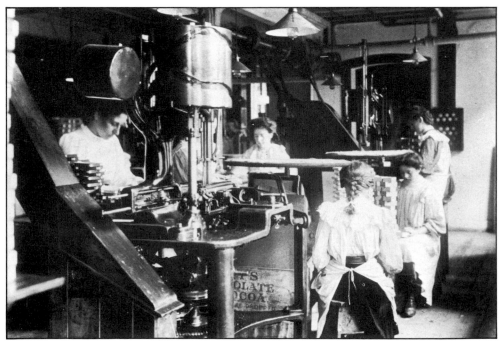

The Wills Memorial Building. *The most striking building erected in Bristol in the twentieth century. Designed in 1911, as Oatley's sketches show, progress was delayed by the First World War. The final account was £501,566 19s. 10d. at 1925 prices. For today's prices multiply by 20.*

Oatley's Grand Scheme. Seen here in an artist's impression drawn by Peter Lawrence, the scheme would have crowned Bristol's tallest hill with an impressive 'castle' to match his 'cathedral'.

George and Harry Wills' munificence. They were both multi-millionaires, men of great integrity, personally amiable and with no particular intellectual interests. But they believed strongly in people who had such interests; and they felt a great social responsibility for the wealth they possessed. Tyndall recalled that Harry Wills remarked to him that they were in a business which, given good management, couldn't help prospering. Wills said, "The way the tobacco business is making money now is positively frightening". They saw in the University a means of doing something useful for Bristol with their money.

It was an aim they pursued in a single-minded and determined, even obstinate, fashion. When the Wills Memorial Building was first proposed, Owen wanted to build in 'modern materials' such as ferro-concrete. George and Harry Wills sought the advice of their architect George (later Sir George) Oatley. Would ferro-concrete last and still be standing in 400 years? Would it last, as the university buildings in Oxford and Cambridge had lasted, they enquired. Oatley replied that it might but that he did not really know the answer as experience of ferro-concrete was limited. The Wills brothers then said, "Well, it shall not be ferro-concrete then. We want something which will be there in 400 years' time".

But though the great 'Cathedral' at the top of Park Street which resulted from their order to Oatley was impressive, the scheme upon which the brothers next embarked was even more striking. A proposal by Tyndall to make a small addition to the 1910 Science buildings in order to house a battery room was resisted by Oatley. Tyndall, perhaps helped by the recent award of the Nobel Prize to Bragg (then of Leeds) persuaded Harry Wills that a new Physics laboratory was needed. Wills acquired Royal Fort House and gardens and gave them to the University as a site. Oatley devised a scheme for a castle-like structure which was to include not only the proposed laboratory but a residential college as well. The scale of the development was enormous. Seven towers each twice the height of the Georgian House were proposed. It was to be an international centre for research and teaching and its towers would "crown the hill overlooking the University".

Royal Fort garden. *A before and after view of Repton's plans for the garden. Some of the trees he planted survived until the 1970s when, sadly, they succumbed to disease.*

Downside. *The estate bought by Harry Wills. Oatley cunningly combined the old house into the new hall of residence as a Warden's house.*

Coombe Dingle. *An old groundsman, Bert Attwell, remembered the first pavilion destroyed by the Suffragettes. It was, he said, about one-third the size of the present structure. Until the 1960s only the present hockey and rugby pitches were used. The rest of the land was laid out as market gardens and hayfields.*

Almost simultaneously George Wills was offering to build a new united hospital for Bristol to amalgamate the Bristol Royal Infirmary and the General Hospital. The site chosen was the one now occupied by the St Monica Home of Rest. But the strong sectarian traditions of the two hospitals proved to be still too strong for amalgamation and the scheme was dropped. Nevertheless the brothers kept acquiring property and giving it to the University. In 1911 George Wills bought the nucleus of the present Athletic Ground at Coombe Dingle. A few years later he added additional acreage. In 1920 he bought the Victoria Rooms and endowed it as a students' union. Harry Wills bought the site of the Stoke Bishop halls of residence in 1922 just before his death.

Such open-handed generosity provoked a kind of envy elsewhere. In 1924 a note about future development at Leeds University (probably written by the acting Vice-Chancellor Jamison) said wistfully "what should we propose to do if such a person as exists probably only in dreams *and at Bristol* were to come along and offer a million of money, provided a satisfactory scheme were produced in (say) fifteen minutes? . . . at present the universities have a tremendous leeway to make up".

The leeway referred to in the Leeds document was caused by the First World War. The new universities met that conflict untried and unfledged. For four years the young men who might reasonably have expected to go to university went instead to the battlefields. Staff too joined the army. It was the thing to do and although some, like Professor Skemp and the Bristol medical student Hardy Parsons found war hateful, they saw it as a duty and paid for it with their lives.

Sorrow at the loss of life and the cruel waste of established scholars and promising students was not the only impact of the war. For the University the loss of staff and the young men meant a financial crisis which could have been exacerbated by the retrenchment ordered by the Government during the war. Fortunately the new universities were able to demonstrate their worth to the country (at Bristol McBain was not only training officers but he also was making important contributions to the study of poison gas and explosives). The Government was sufficiently impressed to undertake to meet the losses in fee income (at that time around 20% of University income) caused by the lack of male students.

When the war ended financial pressures increased. There was a brief boom when student numbers were swollen by the returning soldiers. Their fees increased income but salary costs of returning staff increased expenditure. That problem was heightened by trades union action. Staff salaries had fallen in relative terms and university teachers were joining together in what subsequently became the Association of University Teachers to press their claims for better pay and national scales. Bristol's

Professor McBain, a founder member of the General Executive of the new body and later its President, played a leading role in the campaign.

In a declining economic situation in October 1921, the Government announced that state aid to the universities would be reduced from £1,500,000 to £1,200,000. The universities decided to mount a united appeal to the public for funds but such a complex co-operative initiative proved impossible to implement. Each university was left to go its separate way. The individual appeals were on the whole unsuccessful and had it not been for the support of George and Harry Wills, there would have been a financial crisis in Bristol as there was elsewhere.

But the Government cuts of 1921 were a passing phase, and by 1925 Winston Churchill was able to announce an increase in state aid to universities again. In 1923-24 Bristol with £42 in Treasury grant per student was second only to Sheffield (£48) among the provincial universities in Government support (the average was £37). It also enjoyed considerable local government support and when King George V and Queen Mary came to Bristol on 9 June 1925 to open officially the Wills Memorial Building, they came to a university which was well provided with buildings, in a sound financial condition and which was beginning to show fulfilment of the academic hopes of its founders.

Royal Visit to the University. The King and Queen visited the Victoria Rooms (then the University Union) for lunch where they signed the Visitors' Book with a gold pen.

A loyal mistake. *The plaque commemorating the opening of the Wills Memorial Building.*

Royal Visit. *All Bristol was* en fête *to celebrate the opening of the new building.*

The royal visit and the opening of the building were, rightly, seen as a major event for the city. Loyal citizens, who did not share H. G. Wells' view that the monarch was "uninteresting and alien", lined streets decorated with flags and bunting.

The royal party arrived in Bristol at noon and after a brief but appropriate stop at the Council House, proceeded to luncheon with 75 guests at the Victoria Rooms (given five years earlier by Sir George Wills to serve as the Students' Union for the University).

Haldane, as Chancellor, although he was already ailing (he died in 1928), welcomed the King and Queen in front of the new building and later delivered an address which dwelt upon the aims of a university (which, he decided, should now include provision for adult education).

It was the King himself, politely ignoring the awful solecism of 'George Vth' on the plaque which records the opening, who summed up the feeling of the University and the city at the time.

He said, "The New Buildings of Bristol University are a conspicuous and beautiful landmark in this ancient city, and serve not only to keep fresh the remembrance of a great gift, but also to remind the friends of the University of their obligation to ensure that this gift, so nobly bestowed, be worthily used for the advancement of learning".

The ill-feeling and difficulties between the University College and the Merchant Venturers' College, the trials and tribulations of Cowl's misfortune, the 'honorary degree' scandal and the horrors of the war and its privations were forgotten. The University was happy to acknowledge the magnificent gifts of the **Wills** family, which Cottle and Sherborne later estimated to exceed over £1,250,000 at 1920s prices (worth perhaps 20 times that sum at today's values). It was also happy to accept the royal reminder that its purpose was to advance learning.

Haldane, the University's second Chancellor, *welcomes the King to the University.*

Chapter Four

Discovering a Role

In the period between the wars, although Bristol grew almost not at all in size, its reputation as a centre of learning and research increased, and although the ideas of the founders were no longer perhaps consciously remembered as time removed Lewis Fry and Arrowsmith, Lloyd Morgan and Haldane, real progress in achieving them was made.

In the education of women, for example, Bristol could proudly point to the fact that the first students to qualify in each of the three available categories in dentistry under the Charter were all women (Marjorie Jane White LDS, RCS (Eng) 1915; Violette Bourgeois LDS (Brist) 1919; and Muriel Emma Strode Cash BDS (Brist) 1930). Perhaps more importantly, when in 1920 the University appointed Helen Wodehouse to the Chair of Education, she was one of the first women to hold such a post in a British university. In 1931 the formidable Miss Winifred Lucy Shapland, appointed Secretary of the University in 1928, became the first woman Registrar of any British university – due recognition, if such recognition were needed, that there was more to the education of women than improving their after-dinner conversation.

Haldane's ideas about a 'provincial Charlottenburg' too seemed on its way to fruition. The quality of the work done at Bristol was recognised not only by the election of staff in numbers to Fellowships of the Royal Society, but the way prestigious universities elsewhere sought Bristol staff. In 1926, for example, Professor McBain, who had made striking discoveries in colloid science, after a spell as visiting professor at Berkeley and receiving an Honorary Doctorate from Brown University, Rhode Island, was recruited by Stanford University. Stanford at the same time successfully offered other posts, not only to McBain's leading research collaborator Dr Mary Laing who had won a major international prize in 1924 for her work, but to Miss Norris, Bristol's Chemical Librarian. In 1932 Lennard-Jones moved from a Bristol Physics Chair to a Chair of Chemistry at Cambridge to help create (with J. D. Bernal) a new generation of natural scientists in that university. But perhaps the most outstanding indication of the quality of Bristol's output was the award of the Nobel Prize to the Bristol graduate P. A. M. Dirac for

Chipping Campden. *Erected originally as a game food factory, the buildings were purchased in 1918 by the Board of Agriculture for food preservation work. In 1912 the University assumed responsibility for the Station. British statutory standards for canned foods are based on work carried out at Campden.*

Long Ashton Research Station. *The Station originated in experiments during the 1890s to improve farmhouse cider. These studies were extended by the formation of the National Fruit and Cider Institute. Under the Agricultural Development Act 1909 it became a national agricultural centre and in 1912 the Institute joined the University as its Department of Horticulture and Agriculture. Its interests widened to include willows, crop nutrition and soft fruits. In recent years its responsibilities have changed again and now include research work on cereals and weeds. Open Days impart its information to the agricultural and horticultural community.*

Miss Shapland.

Engineering education. *After the death of Wertheimer in 1924, Engineering education flourished at Unity Street under Andrew Robertson.*

his work in quantum mechanics started at Bristol and completed at Cambridge. (There is an interesting tradition that Dirac was directed into this theoretical work in mathematical physics at Bristol only because he was so inept in the engineering workshops when he was studying for his first degree: the tradition is hardly just either to Dirac or to his professor, Tyndall, who had a well-established record of spotting and encouraging talent and knowing when it could be best developed in different surroundings.)

The successful development of the links with industry desired by some founders was less evident. The Long Ashton Research Station (the University's Department of Horticulture) was certainly doing excellent work in the national development of industrial fruit production, and for the local cider-making and willow industries. According to Sanderson, Nierenstein's work on the biochemistry of cheese-ripening did much for the local Cheddar industry and J. W. McBain's work on the colloid chemistry of soap was not only of national importance to the soap industry but led to Leverhulme's interest in the University. Bristol's supervision of the Campden Research Station virtually created canning as a scientific industry in Britain. The appointment of Arthur Trueman to succeed S. H. Reynolds in the Chair of Geology seemed to augur well for the Somerset coalfields but all Trueman's knowledge could do was to confirm that the coal seams were such that mining would become increasingly more difficult and less economic. Interestingly, Trueman, who left in 1937 to take up a chair in Glasgow and who subsequently became Chairman of the University Grants Committee, was succeeded by W. F. Whittard whose work led to the discovery of alternatives to coal in the West. Whittard broadened the Department's research from its previous stratigraphic and palaeontological concerns into the geology of the south-west approaches, now thought to be a potential source of new oil wealth. (A canyon is named after him off the coast of Brittany.)

Potentially interesting and industrially-linked disciplines, carried over from the Merchant Venturers' College, did not survive the retirement of the holders of the first University chairs although Bristol graduates continued to be in demand in the motor car industry even after Morgan retired from the Automobile Engineering Chair. Appeals to local firms to fund fellowships in return for "full access to research and prior knowledge of the results obtained" seem to have fallen on stony ground and hearts. The decline in local mining may have influenced the decision not to replace Munro in his Chair of Mechanical and Mining Engineering, but in the case of Wertheimer's Chair of Chemical Engineering, the discipline simply had not developed in Bristol. Wertheimer had hoped to establish a Department of Applied Chemistry but the idea had long fallen by the wayside when he died in 1924. In the case of Morgan's Chair of Automobile Engineering,

A. M. Tyndall (left) with P. A. M. Dirac (right) and G. P. Thompson.

Appropriate symbols: the door of the H. H. Wills Physics Laboratory.

there was a feeling that the subject was not quite academically respectable. In the University's defence it must be said that at least the kind of automobiles that lay behind Morgan's teaching were good. He himself had come from Daimler and there was a possibility at one time that the University might acquire a Daimler Chair in Automobile Engineering. His students tended to go to Rolls Royce and Daimler for their work attachments and for their jobs after graduation. Nevertheless, Bristol's association with this discipline was a matter for public criticism by the American educationalist Abraham Flexner. In the British universities, of which on the whole he approved, Flexner discovered nevertheless "such short-sighted and absurd . . . excrescences as the School of Librarianship and course in Journalism at University College, London, the Department of Civic Design at Liverpool and the work in Automobile Engineering at Bristol. This technical development is slight, as compared with that in America, but is none the less deplorable and, we may hope, the defect of youth, for it is of neither liberal nor university quality".

Flexner's attitude was by no means singular. In 1927 Lord Rutherford, opening the Physics Laboratory, told the University that he would view as an unmitigated disaster the utilisation of university laboratories for research bearing on industry.

But though some parts of the University were becoming diffident about relations with industry, the University was certainly not reneging

Extra-Mural Studies: *the University sets up a new department to develop and to enhance the task of bringing the University experience to the people.*

Public Health. *The University and the City combined to improve the health of the citizens.*

on its commitment to the local community. From its first years, University College, Bristol brought higher education to working people, often in their own localities. In 1907 G. H. Leonard, Professor of History, became President of the Bristol Branch of the Workers' Educational Association which replaced the earlier 'Committee to promote the Higher Education of Working Men' on which Leonard had represented the College. When, after the First World War the Government, prompted by Haldane, offered to provide grants to enable universities to establish Departments of Extra-Mural Adult Education, Bristol was already a major focus for such activities, even though they had been limited by the need to be 'self-financing'. In 1924 the University set up its new department with first Hubert Philips, and then J. H. Nicholson (later the first Vice-Chancellor of the University of Hull) as part-time director. In 1926 it established its first resident tutor (W. E. Salt) in the surrounding counties. The regional spread of University work, so often foreshadowed in the speeches of the founders, had become a reality.

But University developments were also having a profound effect in the city of Bristol. In 1909 the City's Medical Officer of Health, Dr David Davies, and Professor Walker Hall had made a major medical breakthrough by establishing firmly the role of the 'carrier' in typhoid outbreaks. Their collaboration continued and was reflected institutionally in 1930 by the setting up of a new University Department of Preventive Medicine in the former men's hall of residence at Canynge Hall. Dr Parry, who had succeeded Davies as City Medical Officer of Health in the same year, became the University's first Professor of Preventive Medicine and, on the retirement of Walker Hall in 1934, became Director of the laboratories for the analysis of bacteriological and pathological specimens. The City and the University laboratories were combined into a joint service at Canynge Hall, and in 1932 the University and the City started training health visitors. The beneficial effect for the ordinary citizens of Bristol of the earlier collaboration and the importance of the new combined arrangements can scarcely be over-emphasised: in 1885 when Davies was appointed, the average age of Bristolians at death was 32 years of age, the general death rate was 23 in 1,000 and the infant mortality rate 165 per 1,000. By 1930 the general death rate had been halved to 11 per 1,000 and the infant mortality rate had fallen to 57 per 1,000.

Though the story of medical co-operation between the University and the City is a happy one at this time, the same cannot be said of relations with the hospitals. In 1919 Sir George Newman, then Chief Medical Officer of the Ministry of Health, conducted a survey of medical schools on behalf of the Government. He found that the London Hospital Schools were the best, while the leading medical schools in the provincial universities were to be found at Manchester and Leeds. Bristol, he told a meeting of University,

The University Song – unheard for years.

Selling the University – a page from a publicity book produced to raise funds for chairs.

Medical Centenary. *The Bristol Medical School celebrated its Centenary with a grand dinner in the Victoria Rooms.*

hospital and medical charity representatives "was great in tradition and in the length of its history, but was not great in all respects . . . it was at sixes and sevens". More precisely the trouble was that it was at the General Hospital *and* the Bristol Royal Infirmary and their continuing rivalry was having an adverse effect on the development of the Medical School. Sir George Wills attempted to break the deadlock by offering to build a new University Hospital on the site now occupied by the St Monica Home of Rest on the Downs if the two hospitals could resolve their differences. Unfortunately they could not and the University Council sought the advice of the eminent surgeon and Professor of Clinical Surgery at Leeds, Sir Berkeley Moynihan. His report highlighted the benefits that could flow from a united hospital system. In particular it would permit the fusion of medical staff and the appointment of full-time clinical professors with "adequate clerical, laboratory and literary assistance" with an allocation of 50–100 hospital beds to each. His report was well received by the University but it was not until June 1940 that the full clinical amalgamation of the hospitals allowed his full recommendations to be implemented.

In 1927 the University Council invited another report – this time from the biologist Sir Patrick Geddes who was beginning to establish a reputation as a town-planner. His brief was essentially structural rather than academic, but the theme he developed, that lines of progress should not be left to chance and the interests of individual donors but should reflect an organised policy towards the needed development of knowledge and education, had academic implications. In his view what Bristol needed was:

(a) A new home for the Medical School on the site eventually used
(b) A faculty building for the Social Sciences on the site now occupied by Senate House
(c) A Faculty of Architecture, Planning and Design where Drama is located in Park Row
(d) An open-air theatre in the Cantocks Close area
(e) An Information Centre
(f) A number of gymnasia "to permit the full recovery of Greek ideals of education"

He also suggested the conversion of old houses into student residences and that the University should help conservation by becoming an agent for the National Trust. Although (or possibly because) Geddes' report, like many reports by academic experts, was a mixture of the already decided (location of the Medical School), the aggrandisement of his own subject (the Faculty of Design), the genuinely far-sighted (the Sports and Information Centres; the concern for student health and accommodation), the inane (the open air theatre) and the impractical (the National Trust), it met with little positive response.

Bristol continued to develop in an organic, unplanned way. In the Arts the strong personality of Felix Boillot helped to lay the foundations of the present School of Modern Languages (it is noteworthy that Bristol's development in this area was cautious and slow when compared with the ready welcome Spanish, Italian and Russian teaching met elsewhere). Boillot, after distinguished war service, figured in the late 1920s in the 'little magazine' movement in Paris centred on Sylvia Beach and Shakespeare and Co. His name appears in their pages along side famous *literati* of the time such as Gide.

Broad, a dominant inter-war figure in Philosophy whose work bridges the gap between Russell and Moore and the later linguistic philosophers, was also a major figure in the Arts Faculty (1920-23) and when he left his work was continued in a sound but unexciting way by Field. Field, a Platonic scholar, wrote a book about the morality of pacifism which was widely read in the 1930s when there was a major peace movement. In 1933 Lewis led the Law Department (created in 1923) into independence as a Faculty. Engineering under Andrew Robertson (Mechanical) and Ferrier and Pippard (Civil) had already developed its characteristic concern to form young engineers who were skilled in mathematics, who were aware of issues wider than engineering and who had enjoyed the opportunity to sample research in a third year project. But the most exciting area of the University in the 1920s and 1930s was undoubtedly the Chemistry and Physics Departments.

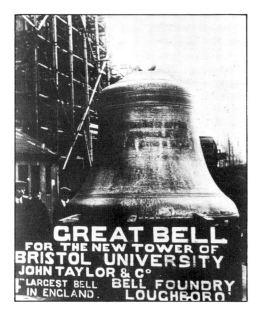

Great George. *The bell that sounds the hours across Bristol. When the Wills Memorial Building was built it was the fourth largest bell in England. It is now the sixth largest and the largest which may be swung on a rope.*

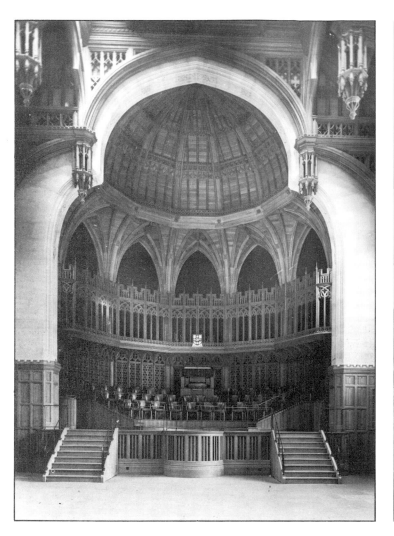

Great Hall: *the carving above the linen-fold panels was particularly fine.*

Great Hall blitzed. *The organ and the fine carving was destroyed.*

Defiant in Disaster. *The Chancellor conferred honorary degrees on the American Ambassador and the Australian Prime Minister the morning after one of the worst raids Bristol suffered during the war.*

Chemistry, where Francis Francis had been joined by Travers and Garner after the departure of McBain, was able to make excellent use of the space, left when Tyndall and his physicists occupied their new building in 1927.

The Physics Department took on a new impetus with the arrival of Nevill Mott from Cambridge. At that time in Britain only Rutherford's Cavendish Laboratory at Cambridge and Bragg's Physics Department at Manchester had international reputations, but the spacious new building to which Mott came in 1933 had already on its staff a future Nobel Laureate in Cecil Powell and among its students Bernard Lovell. They were joined and strengthened by an influx of German scientists fleeing from Hitler's pogroms. Among them was another future Nobel Laureate, Hans Bethe, and a political refugee with strong left-wing views who later became famous for less pleasant reasons – Klaus Fuchs, the 'atom spy'.

Mott and his team laid the foundation of what is now called 'solid state physics'. This, in time, after development during the war-time and some brilliant work in the Bell Telephone Laboratories, led to the development of the transistor and a whole new industry: solid state electronics.

Inevitably, as the decade progressed, the thoughts of the physicists became dominated by the prospect of approaching war. With so many refugees among staff and students, they saw little hope in the peace and disarmament movements of the time. In Physics in 1939 and 1940 Mott recalls that they talked of the possibility of the atomic bomb. In Chemistry, Garner gathered around him a small team to consider the nature of the more conventional explosives which might be required when the conflict came.

Nevill (later Sir Nevill) Mott.

On the outbreak of war, Garner was sent to Fort Halstead in Kent and became Deputy Chief of Armament Research and, later, Chief Superintendent of Armament Research. His large 'extra-mural' explosives research team continued to operate in Bristol and he returned to Bristol on Fridays, lectured to his students on Saturday morning and spent the rest of the weekend on departmental matters before returning to Kent on Sunday afternoon. The Physics building became the home of the 'Sutton Group' working on the klystron and magnetron valves, (the latter a brilliant breakthrough by Randall and Boot at Birmingham), a vital component in radar and target-finding aids to bombing. The skill of J. H. Burrow as a glass-blower solved some of the recalcitrant detailed problems of the valve which was considered by the Americans more than adequate return for all that they sent to Britain in war *materiel* under 'Lend-lease'.

Lovell was also involved in this work elsewhere in the country, and it fell to Charles Frank (later Professor of Physics at Bristol but at the time seconded from Oxford) to make one of the most significant scientific intelligence breakthroughs of the war – the spotting of the first German radar station at Auderville. Another future Bristol Physics Professor, Peter Fowler, then a young RAF officer, used his radar scanner to direct bombers to

Professor W. E. Garner.

Professor Roderick Collar, Vice-Chancellor 1968-69.

Charles (later Sir Charles) Frank.

destroy a major German jamming device at the Feldberg near Frankfurt. Mott led a team trying to work out the probable range of the German V2 rockets and a future Mathematics Professor, Leslie Howarth, devised the formula which enabled points of impact to be determined from V2 shock waves. The future Professor of Aeronautical Engineering, Roderick Collar, solved the problem of vibration on Barnes Wallis' famous bouncing bomb and solved a key problem which had caused the deaths of many experienced pilots in the early days of night fighting. The problem was a perceptual one. The pilots believed they were climbing when in fact they were diving. Flying by instruments alone, not 'by the seat of the pants', provided the solution. A team led by Alfred Pugsley solved problems of 'flutter' in Spitfire wings.

Bristol's war record was by no means unique. All over the country the 'new' universities, now dubbed the 'red brick universities' after the title of Bruce Truscot's 1945 book, made contributions based on the expertise built up in the inter-war period. The country recognised that once again the universities had proved their value in war; and once again the universities hoped to reap the rewards of their virtue in the peace.

The divisions which marked, and marred, the early progress of the University in the immediate post-Charter years had disappeared by 1945. Thomas Loveday succeeded Isambard Owen as Vice-Chancellor in 1922 after a short inter-regnum when Professor Francis held the post in an acting capacity. The appointment of a Vice-Chancellor is a complex business involving many hands but in 1963 Loveday recorded his own recollection of how he was offered the post. Haldane invited him to dinner at his London home. Loveday recalled that Haldane said to him, "I hope you will like this", and offered him a dish of tripe and the Vice-Chancellorship. He liked the latter but found the former only barely tolerable. Loveday was a member of an old Oxfordshire county family with special county interests. His own rural interests enabled him to establish happy relationships for the University with the surrounding rural counties of Gloucestershire, Somerset, and Wiltshire and those who guided their destinies. More importantly too he shared interests in gardens with Sir Stanley Badock, who succeeded Sir George Wills as Chairman of Council, and Hiatt Baker, who succeeded J. W. Arrowsmith as Chairman of the General Purposes Committee. These personal interests enabled him to secure and maintain the full confidence of Council and thus avoid the difficulties that previously existed between Senate and Council.

For example, Tyndall recalled that when his predecessor in the Chair of Physics retired, the matter was discussed independently by two separate committees of Senate and Council respectively on the grounds that while Senate had to report on the question, the election to the Chair was Council's responsibility. The two short lists did not agree and the result was that no appointment was made for some time. Loveday established a scheme by

Winston Churchill and Thomas Loveday, *the third Chancellor with the third Vice-Chancellor.*

which Joint Senate and Council Committees were appointed to deal with such matters. All cause for conflict between lay and academic members was thus removed. The lay members themselves no longer divided on political or sectarian grounds. Even the old emnities at the hospitals had been buried. The partial destruction by enemy action of the Wills Building and the defiant speech made by the University's Chancellor Winston Churchill soon after the fires were put out seemed to emphasise the University's oneness with the bomb-damaged city. In retrospect Loveday's Vice-Chancellorship can be seen as a period in which the University achieved unity, purpose and reputation.

Although he had passed retiring age, Loveday stayed on as Vice-Chancellor to the end of the war. The University then offered the Vice-Chancellorship to Philip Morris, and it was under his guidance that the University met the difficulties, challenges and opportunities afforded by the next 20 years in which the universities enjoyed unprecedented public support and esteem.

Chapter Five

The Years of Expansion

In some ways the appointment of Philip Morris as Vice-Chancellor of a university like Bristol may seem extraordinary. He had never taught in a university, and in his entire working life he wrote only one book. He himself said he was not a master of anything. He had been a training college lecturer, and an administrator with the Kent Education Authority. After Army service early in the Second World War, in 1944 he went to the Ministry of Education to devise an Adult Education plan which would prepare the thousands of men and women about to be demobilised for civilian life in post-war Britain. These tasks, all successfully accomplished, reveal the man. He was a very able administrator, a gifted chairman, a man who could combine idealism with a sharp sense of practical ways forward, a planner with vision.

Philip (later Sir Philip) Morris.

As Roger Wilson noted in a memorial address, "Morris' vision of education was total. He saw schools, universities, training colleges, colleges of technology at any level, adult education, all as a continuous whole. He rejected the concept of mere usefulness". "The biggest single issue of modern times", Morris wrote, "is that men and women will content themselves with an unthinking capitulation to what seem to be the insistent demands of the immediate present". For Morris the answer lay in educational institutions alive with the movement and enjoyment of human thought, communities "groping for the wisdom that would make life more than its possessions and hierarchies". Universities were to be "the nursing mothers of the men, women and values and ideas that are needed to sustain a free, responsible society, guided by light and truth rather than by makeshifts and possessions". In short, Morris wished to return to the Arnoldian ideas of "sweetness and light" which had inspired the founders of University College, Bristol.

Morris saw that planning would be needed but that the plan required went beyond the needs of only Bristol as a university. The right plan would have national and international aspects and had implications for all disciplines. But Morris was also an administrator who saw that even the grandest design required attention to detail. As far as universities were concerned that meant teachers and one of his first and most successfully

accomplished tasks was to attract good people to Bristol. In some cases appointments were made at lecturer level and, as funds became available through expansion later, promotions were made to chairs. In others the senior appointments came first and the professors attracted gifted assistants and postgraduate researchers. The measure of Morris' success could be seen in department after department across the University. In discipline after discipline, Bristol scholars emerged who were among the national, and in many cases, the international leaders of their subject. Frank, who joined Mott and Powell at Physics; Kitto in Classics; L. C. Knights and then Frank Kermode in English; Leslie Howarth in Mathematics; Collar, Pugsley and Rawcliffe in Engineering; Neale in Child Health, all were appointed around this time. Others, like Hinton (Entomology) and Körner (Philosophy), were promoted to chairs later. There were still others who, like the Ancient Historian Arnaldo Momigliano, came to Bristol for a time before accepting chairs in other universities.

To include all the names would make this account tedious; one may say, simply, that in the first ten years or so of Morris' Vice-Chancellorship, Bristol changed from being a good provincial university with some outstanding departments into a university with an excellent international reputation in virtually every discipline it pursued.

The Veterinary School at Langford. *One of Bristol's best post-war achievements was the rapid construction of a new veterinary school. Associated institutes like the Meat Research Institute carry on Bristol's traditional interest in improving the nation's food.*

Professor Shepherdson. *Bristol has been fortunate in the quality of its mathematicians. Shepherdson, for example, was appointed a lecturer when he was only 19. Although a new School of Mathematics and Computer Building was erected, almost before it was completed it was already too small for the numbers of students who wanted to study Mathematics and its related disciplines such as Computer Science.*

The School of Education. *Philip Morris' great achievement was his encouragement of Education as a discipline. Its Berkeley Square building is named after Helen Wodehouse.*

The Alfred Marshall Building. *A speculative architectural intrusion in Berkeley Square, many regret that the building named in honour of the first Principal of University College, Bristol is not more distinguished.*

The Psychology Building. *The gracious entrance to the Psychology Department is much in demand by film companies.*

The physical expansion of the University implied by these appointments was not readily accomplished at a time of great national shortage of money and materials, when new planning laws and government licences and permits stood in the way of desirable progress. For example, the Government readily accepted the recommendations of the Loveday Committee that the country needed additional veterinary schools, and Bristol happily accepted the responsibility of becoming one of the new veterinary centres. But the task of building a new veterinary school, providing academic and research facilities, sometimes literally only months ahead of the first student intake which was to use them, taxed even Morris' considerable powers of diplomacy, tact and cajolery. In building their memorial to their father, the Wills brothers had asked George Oatley to build for 400 years; the architects employed by the University in the late 1940s and early 1950s could have no such perspectives. The University had to build what was necessary with what was available and if the buildings which arose at that time at Langford and Park Row lack style, then the exigencies of the post-war period are the reason and the excuse.

As the 1950s progressed the nation seemed a little more prosperous and building plans could be more considered. New buildings for Medicine and Engineering were provided on St Michael's Hill. Both buildings had beneficial effects beyond the subjects directly involved. Geography was enabled to expand by taking over the old medical premises in University Road and the abandonment of the Unity Street buildings ended the uneasy relationship between the Faculty of Engineering and its host the Merchant Venturers' College. The link between the Deanship of the Engineering Faculty and the Principalship of the Merchant Venturers' College (established to protect Wertheimer's personal position in 1909) had been broken in 1949. Now the College had the space to become first a College of Advanced Technology and then, in a series of transformation scenes, the University of Bath and the nucleus of Bristol Polytechnic.

A major new building for Chemistry was also planned and built. The work of Courtaulds' Technical Services Section architecturally, it was, in the words of Pevsner, "the University's first venture into the international style" and, as such, perhaps an appropriate permanent symbol of its new international standing. The School of Chemistry and the other University buildings on the slopes of St Michael's Hill were not, however, universally welcomed. The area had not been densely populated and the majority of the houses which had stood on the site were of little architectural merit and were in poor condition. The City Council was happy to exercise its compulsory purchase powers on the University's behalf. But some of the displaced inhabitants were also parishioners of St Michael's on the Mount Without where the vicar was a local Labour politician, Alderman the Reverend F. C. Vyvyan-Jones. In speeches in the City Council and through the press he

Royal Visit. *Sir Philip Morris greets Her Majesty the Queen. In attendance is Alec Forrest, the first member of the University's staff to be appointed a Judge.*

Clifton Hill girls, *the first to benefit from hall life. In 1936 the UGC reported, "As compared with lodgings or with many homes, a hall offers an environment where intellectual interests are strong. It offers students exceptionally favourable opportunities for the stimulating interplay of mind with mind, for the formation of friendships, and for learning the art of understanding and living with others of outlook and temperament unlike their own. It can be, and it often is, a great humanising force".*

Mortimer House: *the Warden sat by the little table and fined any inmate who was out late 3d.*

Canynge Hall: *eating together was a 'humanising force'; their favourite food was fried bread, called 'sliders'.*

Wills Hall: *a daring, illegal 'sausage-sizzle', a kind of gas-fire barbecue.*

Manor Hall: *'humanising' young women also meant eating together.*

Hall Warden. *Usually men of military experience. In the women's halls, experienced school teachers were preferred.*

Hall Life *was occasionally enlivened by Rags – at Burwalls, for example, flinging the statue of a boy into the pond of the neighbouring Hiatt Baker Garden. Retrieving the statue was a long and smelly business.*

managed to focus on the University some of the resentment ordinary Bristolians felt at the transformation of the war-damaged but still recognisable old pre-war city into the brave new world of the urban planners.

The University's problem was exacerbated by its connection through the Medical Faculty with the National Health Service. The NHS was starting to build a new major city centre hospital in Bristol just as it was in many other major British cities at the time. The difficulty in Bristol was that the hospital chosen was the Bristol Royal Infirmary and the selected site, to the east of St Michael's Hill, was also part of Alderman Vyvyan-Jones' parish.

The University felt a little hard done by. The buildings in question were essential and the alternative, which had been considered just after the war – to move the University to an entirely new site at the Ashton Court Mansion – would have been more destructive of a valuable city asset. The University's post-war development had helped the city. The benefits of having a large teaching hospital in Bristol were unquestionable. The University's intervention in the creation of the Bristol Old Vic, and its associated theatre school, had been decisive. The Old Vic Company, the sadly short-lived Western Theatre Ballet, and the creation of Drama and Music Departments in the University had given the city a vital cultural impetus.

Moreover, one group of University buildings which was the cause of specific complaint – two new blocks built by speculators in Berkeley Square and leased to the University – one of which was used to house the Education Department for which the historic Royal Fort House had proved to be too small. The enormous expansion of Education under Morris' Vice-Chancellorship, which culminated some years later (1969) in it attaining Faculty status, represented visible evidence of the commitment he wanted Bristol and other universities to make to the training of teachers. Morris placed enormous importance on the schools and the quality of what they taught because all the population would in time pass through them. The national role of the universities, who already determined much of what was taught through the 'O' and 'A' level examinations (virtually invented by Morris when he was in the Ministry of Education), was to ensure the quality of the teachers. The growth of Education in the University manifested itself in Bristol and the surrounding region through the Institute of Education, a constitutional device which established formal links between the University and the training colleges in Bristol, Bath, Cheltenham and Gloucester. Bristol and the region stood to benefit from the teachers produced by the Institute and by the in-service training facilities the Institute developed.

But Bristolians were not able to see the cultural and educational benefits. They could only see the changing of an old architectural order and resent it.

After the Ball. *Dances, formal and informal, were a necessary way of meeting the opposite sex – for girls, climbing while dressed in a ball gown into hall after a late night posed special problems.*

Hall Life. *Common rooms were the centre of hall life, but they were often the still centre of a turning world.*

A Growing University. *An aerial view taken just after the completion of the Queen's Building. Alderman Vyvyan-Jones' parish was still more or less intact.*

The city was losing its pride in its University. But it would be wrong to suppose that the University of Bristol was unique in this loss of local support. The same national forces – hospitals, university buildings in the city centre site, new architecture for old – had the same effects elsewhere. Edinburgh University, for example, was criticised for its treatment of George Square and The Queen's University, Belfast, was attacked for destroying an old terrace of houses called Queen's Elms.

The loss of local support was made worse by the loss of local students. The minutes of the Education Committee of the City and County of Bristol reveal that in the 1930s, the last comparable 'normal' time in higher education since in the late 1940s student numbers were swollen and distorted by returning soldiers, scholarship awards were made to students to enable them to study (with very few exceptions) in three universities only – Oxford, Cambridge and Bristol. The bulk of the awards went to local students of the local university. In the 1950s this changed. The Government indicated that it would give support to local authorities which gave grants to enable students to study anywhere in the national system of universities. Locally, Bristol University began to be viewed by Bristolians as an alien 'intellectual colony' but nationally students were now to enjoy, at public expense, the academic freedom of *Lernfreiheit,* the right to choose their subjects and their teachers and to travel to be taught where their chosen teacher was in residence.

This continental freedom, observed by Haldane, Ramsay and others as a feature of the German system they admired, had, perhaps significantly, never been pursued by them. It soon became clear that the new freedom was imposing new strains on the universities. From its very first years as a University, Bristol had recognised a need to make provision for student accommodation. Clifton Hill had been opened as the University's first hall of residence for women within a year or two of the Charter. After some temporary expedients at Mortimer House in Clifton and Canynge Hall, the first purpose-built hall for men, Wills Hall, opened in 1929. Manor Hall for women opened around the same time and these Halls, plus some lodgings (or digs as they were called then) sufficed to meet the need for accommodation. Until the middle 1950s most students were still able to live at home. But the new influx of students from all over the country gradually began to swamp the existing arrangements for accommodation. The applications for admission began also to swamp the universities' administrative arrangements.

At this crucial stage, Morris became Chairman of the Committee of Vice-Chancellors and Principals. The Committee had its origins in the informal body called by Ramsay and Hicks in the 1880s, but in the form in which it existed in the 1950s (and exists now) it dated back to 1922. It is often thought of, and indeed spoken to and listened to by Government ministers, as if it were the authentic single national voice of the universities. But it was (and is) not that: it was (and is) simply what its names states: the Committee of Vice-Chancellors and Principals of the British universities. In the middle 1950s, when Morris was Chairman, it was rendered almost incapable of unified action by the perception, widely shared among its members, that the strength of the individual universities lay in their individual hard won 'autonomy'. As Wilson observed, "It took all Philip Morris' strength as chairman to persuade them to see that they must work together to evolve positive forward-looking policies for the hurricane of demographic, political and social forces that would burst on the universities in the sixties if they were to sustain their freedom even in such matters as admission policies and procedures, and good husbandry of scarce resources, and not have answers thrust upon them". Morris happily succeeded, with the result that the Universities Central Council on Admissions was in place when the post-war baby boom manifested itself in higher education in the early 1960s. Just as importantly, the Vice-Chancellors were able to convince the Government of the need to do something about student accommodation. Thus the decade in Bristol which witnessed the building of Churchill Hall, Hiatt Baker and Badock Halls with extensions to existing Halls saw other, and very similar halls, created in other universities. The creation of the halls of residence was more than a simple response to a perceived problem; in Bristol and other universities it was seen as a desirable change in the nature of the University.

Wills Hall.

The Society of Merchant Venturers.
When the Queen's Building was opened, the opportunity was taken to place on record the Merchant Venturers' contribution to sustaining the Faculty of Engineering. The Society helped the University in other ways. It agreed to sell Manor House, Richmond House, Clifton Place and Rivers Cottage for use as students' hostels and provided financial help for other halls and for the founding of the Law Faculty. Several Masters of the Society have served with distinction on the University Council.

Exercises in modern international style. *The University Union Building was planned for a University of 10,000 students. The School of Chemistry was built right across what early University planners hoped would be a grand ceremonial staircase leading from Park Row to the Royal Fort gardens.*

The Dental Hospital. *After much agonising about a site, including considering Canynge Hall, the University eventually developed its Dental Hospital close to the BRI in Lower Maudlin Street.*

Residence was seen as an important part of the university experience of a student, and when, in the late 1950s and early 1960s, it was thought necessary to create new universities all revealed themselves attached to the residential ideal. In some, such as Lancaster, Kent and York, this took the form of re-inventing the collegiate system of Oxbridge.

The change in philosophy and the new universities to implement it were enshrined in the Robbins Report of 1963 which the Conservative Government adopted without significant debate. (It is suggested in Macmillan's memoirs that this was due less to a desire for enlightenment in higher education than to enlightened self-interest in a cabinet thrown into a leadership struggle by the Prime Minister's indisposition.) After the 1964 election the incoming Labour Government under Harold Wilson was even more committed to the universities. The new Prime Minister wanted to release the 'white heat of the technological revolution' (a singularly inappropriate metaphor to apply to new technology however important it may be to traditional steel-making). He also, with Jenny Lee, founded something which he called 'the University of the Air' and which subsequently became known as 'The Open University'. The aim of this revolutionary new concept in higher education – to bring the university experience to the masses, the artisans, women and the educationally disadvantaged – was almost exactly that which had motivated Percival, Jowett and others to found the University College 90 years earlier.

The goodwill of successive governments produced a rash of new universities across the country. Like the new universities of 50 years earlier they almost immediately attracted unfavourable press and public comment about their practices and precepts. But universities like Bristol, now regarded as 'older' or 'traditional' universities, benefited, by contrast, in public esteem without losing their share of government *largesse*. Bristol embarked on a period of academic expansion. While there were developments on the Science and Engineering side of the University such as a new Department of Inorganic Chemistry (produced by splitting the existing Department of Physical and Inorganic Chemistry in 1964) and Biochemistry, the bulk of new developments at Bristol came on the 'Arts' side of the University. The jewel in the crown was Drama. Founded as a discipline in 1946 with Taig as first lecturer, it had grown under the leadership of Glynne Wickham (Chair in 1960) in size and reputation. Productions in its studio theatre in the Wills Memorial Building (1951-67) stimulated national interest and Bristol's lead in founding the subject as a university discipline was followed elsewhere. Within the University itself, it stimulated an interest in dramatic literature in performance, and a concern for the dramatic literature of a culture which is now clearly seen as characteristic of Bristol's teaching of Arts disciplines such as Classics and Modern Languages. In particular the French Department has established a reputation for foreign language productions.

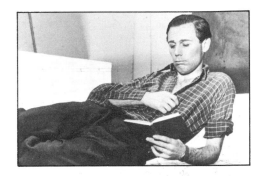

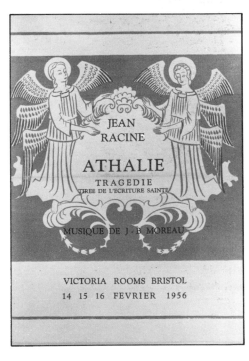

Drama. *In the Drama Department, in Classical and Modern Languages and in the Union, Bristol established a high reputation for drama.*

The Bristol Old Vic. *Dorothy Tutin and Emrys Jones in* As You Like It. *In 1946 Sir Philip Morris became Chairman of the new company formed to run the Theatre Royal. He was succeeded as Chairman by another Vice-Chancellor, Sir Alec Merrison. The company, and the University Theatre Collection, has inherited the London Old Vic's archives.*

Royal Visit. *Princess Marina, Duchess of Kent, at the opening of the Vandyck (now Glynne Wickham) Theatre. Beside her Alderman Vyvyan-Jones, a vigorous opponent of the University's new buildings.*

Other new departments such as Theology, Sociology, Politics and Social and Economic History were founded, in some cases *ab initio,* in others by a process of fission from an existing department. There was considerable innovation. Bristol was the first university to establish Econometrics as a separate discipline and was among the first to establish a Chair of Accounting. The Social Sciences disciplines founded in the late 1950s and early 1960s were organised into a separate Faculty in 1966.

The way students were taught was also changing. Bristol had pioneered a three-subject degree in the 1920s and 1930s for those who wanted a broader curriculum similar to the Scottish pass degree, but its example had not been widely followed. Even in Bristol itself there were now fewer pass degree subjects and most Honours students followed courses leading to a degree in a single subject. In the 1960s, however, there was an enormous growth of two-subject degrees or Joint Schools. Apart from offering the broader education many favoured, small new departments found them easier to teach in a credible fashion.

When Sir Philip Morris retired in 1966 he could look back on 20 years in which the University had almost trebled in size, which saw the foundation laid for two new Faculties, the birth of several new Departments and the construction of a wide range of new buildings. A new School of Veterinary Science and a new School of Architecture had been created. The education students received was broader, by discipline, by culture, by residence. Even if nationally the universities' response to his call to educate teachers had been only half-hearted, other matters, such as the Universities Central Council on Admissions, had gone very well and the English, and indeed Commonwealth, university system he left was certainly better than the one he found. It must have seemed to him as he handed over to Professor John Harris, his successor, that the course for Bristol and the course for the universities nationally was set fair.

But in fact it was not to be. The Wilson Government had set its expectations of the university system unrealistically high and the time-scale in which to deliver the goods expected was unrealistically short. As the Labour Government looked for public expenditure cuts, its eye fell on the universities and it found them wanting. Education Minister Shirley Williams listed her causes for concern in 'Thirteen Points'. They covered such matters as two year degrees, the balance between 'Arts' and 'Science', the numbers of overseas students. By and large, they were ignored by the universities, but nevertheless they proved to be essentially the agenda for discussion between successive governments and the universities for the next 15 years.

The Government's manifest disappointment set the universities a problem. The chance of two world wars had enabled them to demonstrate their worth and usefulness in clear-cut and dramatic ways. As the decade drew to a close, the cynical in the universities were vaguely aware they needed a war: as the 1960s ended, they found themselves caught up in a revolution.

John Harris.

Student Revolt: *the red dawn of an age of revolution.*

Chapter Six

The Difficult Years

The student revolution started, in Bristol at least, with an event which, in its declared aims, closely resembled the ideas of the founders a hundred years earlier. It was called 'The Free University' and the idea was to offer higher education to which no test of age, religion, sex, attainment or finance barred entry. In practice it was a series of loosely-connected open discussions on topics such as 'Options and choices in university courses'. At the outset the tone of its discussions was mildly reformist but after about a week the organising committee produced a French student at a meeting in the Winston Hall of the new Students' Union building. The student in question does not appear to have said or done anything very much but the mere fact of his appearance changed the character of 'The Free University'.

At that time (June 1968) students in France and Germany were involved in major confrontations on the streets. In France the situation was so serious that President de Gaulle believed that *les événements,* as they were called, would result in a *coup.* His view was widely shared, and British newspapers of the time were full of speculation that a combination of students and workers would bring down the Fifth Republic. The presence at Bristol's 'Free University' of one who seemed to be actually tearing down the capitalist system while Bristol students were content to discuss syllabus reform was electrifying. The 'Free University' discussion suddenly became focussed sharply on the hunt for provocation by the University authorities (perhaps the first time that students thought of senior members of the University in that way). There was some difficulty in finding a suitable issue but as the debate wore on it was provided by the Union's own workers. The porters, not unreasonably, wanted to go home and asked the meeting to end at the agreed time of 10.30 pm. The issue became 'Do we control our own Union or not?' and Bristol's first sit-in began.

The sit-in at the Union lasted through the weekend. By then it was plain, even to the most revolutionary-minded, that this was not a particularly effective or even daring challenge to authority. This view was confirmed when the Vice-Chancellor, Professor John Harris, returned from a

Students on the March: *in the 1920s students marched in procession to the Cathedral for the beginning of term service.*

Students on the March: *in the 1960s they discovered they could march in the service of mammon: the Anderson report called for higher student grants.*

Storming the Barricades. *Peter Lawrence's adaptation of the famous French revolutionary picture had a changed slogan – Liberté, Egalité, Maternité – the issue was the University Nursery, the ad hoc committee the appropriately named NAG (Nursery Action Group).*

conference he had been attending. He announced that he regarded the sit-in as a matter for the Union Council. The Union was to control its own affairs.

This cool unflustered reaction was typical of Professor Harris. Appointed to the Chair of Zoology in 1944, he succeeded Sir Philip Morris as Vice-Chancellor in 1966. Sadly, the University would enjoy the benefit of his leadership for only another week. He collapsed and died in his office. When 'the revolution' resumed in the late Autumn term, Roderick Collar, Professor of Aeronautical Engineering, was Vice-Chancellor, having been appointed for a single year while a permanent appointment was being made.

The issue now was 'reciprocal membership' of the Union. In essence this meant opening the University Union to all students in Bristol. In practice it meant little. Few students on the scattered sites of the Bristol Polytechnic, or of the training colleges at Redland or Fishponds would find it convenient to use the building in Queen's Road on a regular basis. But this did not trouble the proponents of confrontation. They were not interested in real situations of usage or of licensing laws and the like. As Paul Vollans, President of the Union, said, around 70 students "were prepared to sit in on any issue anywhere".

At crowded Union General Meetings in October and November the 'Free University' Committee carried resolutions insisting on reciprocal membership immediately. Through the Union's constitutional committee procedure Vollans and his colleagues decided on a working party to consider the genuine legal and other problems. The University had already identified a working party as being the best way to discuss the issue. The Union Officers and the University met to discuss a solution in the Union's Finance Committee at 5 pm on 5 December. Had the matter been left in the hands of the duly elected committees there seems little doubt that the student officers and the University authorities could have reached a satisfactory proposal to place before the Union membership early in the Spring term. An *ad hoc* committee, however, typical of many such groups which flourished in succeeding years, approached the University authorities seeking permission for a lobby of students to be admitted to the Senate House on the occasion of the Union Officers' committee meeting. The University authorities agreed to the lobby and even agreed to permit representatives of the lobby to attend the meeting as observers. Instead of the few dozen University students expected, several hundred students (and a few people who had never been students) turned up and the Union's Finance Committee found itself discussing a sensitive and difficult issue in very intimidating circumstances. But the student officers and the University authorities did agree to set up a joint working party which would make a proposal which would be put to a referendum of all the students early in the New Year. Their decision was conveyed to the lobby of students, who by then had revealed their true intentions. There was to be an occupation of the Senate House. Locked doors were forced open and students occupied all sections of the building, with the exception of the Vice-Chancellor's office. The demands by the sit-in quickly escalated.

This sit-in lasted 11 days and, since such events in British universities had up to that time been rare, British journalists, frantically seeking for another and more convenient Paris, flocked to the scene. For a time education correspondents enjoyed almost the status of war correspondents as they reported from the Bristol barricades. Certainly, there was an element of truth (with due allowance for hyperbole) in John Grigg's remark *(The Guardian* 6.2.69) that in December 1968 'the eyes of the nation were upon Bristol University'.

What the nation saw was not particularly illuminating at Bristol or anywhere else where such events occurred. Reporters tended to see what they hoped to see, a reflection of the 'French revolution' – only in Belfast, where a student group called 'People's Democracy' was a major cause of the events that led to the tragic history of Northern Ireland in the last 15 years, could such a view have been justified and the British press, at that time, was not interested in Ulster's affairs. Unfortunately for the universities, the

Drama. *Normal life goes on.*

A statue of a Vice-Chancellor – *a tribute on the lawn opposite Senate House.*

Rugby at Twickenham. *Bristol defeated Durham to win the University Athletic Union championship.*

inaccurate view purveyed through the press of the 'student revolution of 1968' is the one which has persisted and the resulting damage done to the university system as a whole has been considerable.

The reality of the situation in Bristol was that the sit-in enjoyed little student support. It was roundly condemned by the Union General Meeting (the sovereign body of the Union) and by students in other Bristol colleges. The academic staff's professional ability to see all sides of any question led them to a more equivocal response: they passed a resolution saying they sympathised with the sit-in's aims while deploring its methods.

In fact there was nothing in the sit-in's aims that warranted even this timorous level of support. Bristol was not a reactionary university. It had recognised early on in the 1960s expansion that such a great and sudden increase in staff and in students would produce strains. A Senate Committee chaired by Professor Frank had looked at the details of departmental organisation with a view to widening the responsibilities for academic decisions. This was partly a response to an AUT paper *Democracy or oligarchy* sponsored by Professor Dickinson. In 1966 assistant lecturers were admitted to membership of Faculty Boards and in the same year another Senate committee was set up under Professor Ashworth to consider how the University administered its academic affairs. When the new Students' Union building was opened in 1966 there was a review of the Union constitution which gave the students a wide measure of autonomy in the conduct of their own affairs. In June 1968 the University Council gave approval to a proposal to appoint student representatives to six major committees of the University.

University Orchestra.

Nor was the University's response to the student protest when it came reactionary. The working party on reciprocal membership duly reported and its recommendations were implemented. This did nothing to mollify the 'revolutionaries'. Their protest issue was now 'victimisation' – the cases of the 37 students who faced student discipline charges arising out of the occupation of Senate House. Eleven cases were dismissed for lack of evidence and 26 others, despite local and national press calls for massive retribution, were only required to sign an undertaking against further disruptive practices. Senate also set up a committee under Dr. A. A. O. Morrison to see what lessons could be learnt. When the Morrison Committee and the Ashworth Committee reported in June 1969 their recommendations were speedily adopted.

The Morrison Committee report's main conclusion was that, despite the efforts to broaden participation in academic decision-making, confidentiality in conducting the University's business had been carried too far and could well be relaxed. As part of the process of relaxation Morrison suggested that an Information Office should be set up. In this, the Committee's report went beyond Geddes' earlier 1920s suggestion. The sit-in and the events that surrounded it had produced mountains of leaflets, pamphlets and broadsheets

The University Library. *The University College started without a library and the first attempt to create one was described as a cupboard with a few books in it kept by Professor Rowley who was accorded the title of Honorary Librarian in 1888. In 1901 when he was succeeded in that capacity by Ernest Sibree, the entire library catalogue could be contained in one volume. By then various departments in the University College had begun to keep their own libraries. In 1911 the Medical Library was moved to the East Wing of the Blind Asylum and the Arts Library to the Blind Asylum Chapel. In 1913 the Arts Library moved to the Drill Hall. Reading conditions were difficult and many students preferred to use the City Library at College Green. In 1923 the University appointed its first full-time Librarian, W. Luther Cooper, who was able to take up his duties in the fine new Library – a version of a Tudor Great Hall by George Oatley – in the New Buildings, as the Wills Memorial Building was then called. When F. L. Kent succeeded Cooper in 1946 he found that the departmental libraries had developed strongly but independently. He predicted that a federal library system would be needed. When, in the late 1950s the University libraries, like many other University services, were being swamped by rising demand the wisdom of Kent's view was manifest and it fell to his successor, James Shum Cox (1951-66), to implement it. The Library Headquarters in the Wills Memorial Building was extended*

The First Library *in what is now the Geography Lecture Theatre.*

The Wills Memorial Building Library.

The University Library: *Twist and Whitley's new headquarters building.*

but even with this addition the system could not cope with demand. Under Norman Higham, the first Bristol Librarian to be elected President of the Library Association, the Library Headquarters moved to a new building by Twist and Whitley in Tyndall Avenue. During its history the University continually built up its collection of books and periodicals but it also acquired historical and special bibliographical treasures. The most interesting historical records are the papers of Isambard Kingdom Brunel and the family records of the slave-owning Pinney family. Perhaps chief among the bibliographical collection is the copy of the Nüremberg Chronicle printed in 1496. The Bristol copy is one of the very few which still contains the pages relating to the reign of Pope Joan.

Theatre Collection. *A library with a difference, Britain's only fully catalogued theatre collection contains the archives of the Victorian actor manager Herbert Beerbohm Tree, and drawings, set designs of both national and local importance. Among the most attractive is this pantomime costume used at Bristol's Prince's Theatre which stood beside the University's first buildings.*

The Cobden Book of Hours. *In 1977 the University Library acquired the Library of the National Liberal Club. It was thought that the chief value of this collection was its unique sets of election addresses but among the books there was what appeared to be, from its binding, a mid-nineteenth century book. On inspection it proved to be a beautiful mediaeval Book of Hours, previously the property of Richard Cobden.*

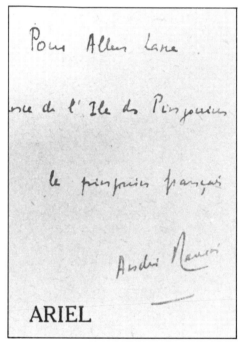

plus a few short-lived newspapers with names like *Offensive, Open Conspiracy, Red Mole* and *Black Dwarf*. Many of these were deliberately scatological and made a point of obscene and personal attacks on named members of staff. Their chief aim was, as Marcuse, the American philosopher they favoured, put it, "to rip the mask from violence". In other words, it was to undermine legitimate authority and, if possible, behave in such a fashion that legitimacy could be asserted only by a use of force which in turn would be used by the protestors to sanctify and justify further and more violent actions. At the height of the Bristol problems Professor Chambers produced a series of unofficial news-sheets. In most cases the news-sheet consisted of a cyclostyled single typed sheet. Modest as the news-sheet was, it was found to be very effective in combating the 'black propaganda' of the protestors. Morrison wanted the news-sheet to be continued on a regular and professional basis. This and other major recommendations were adopted immediately; some minor points were referred to the new Vice-Chancellor.

Professor Collar's temporary and turbulent tenure of the Vice-Chancellorship ended in September 1969 with the arrival of Professor Harris' successor Dr (later Sir) Alec Merrison. His appointment as Vice-Chancellor was not Dr Merrison's first acquaintance with Bristol. By the chance of war, as an undergraduate at King's College, London, he had been evacuated to

Penguin No 1. *Before his death, Sir Allen Lane presented the University with his personal collection of Penguin books, most of them signed by their authors. His successors at Penguin Books have continued to deposit copies as new books are produced. Paper-back publication revolutionised British intellectual life: the University is particularly proud to have this collection in memory of a man who led that revolution.*

University Finance. *The five-year forward planning period for University finance known as the quinquennial system was ended by the Labour Government. Successive governments continued to believe that the support they offered was generous but universities felt they could no longer see where they were going. The Newsletter cartoon is by Peter Lawrence.*

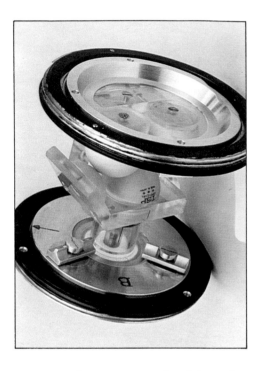

Spacelab. *Bristol experiments about how solids and liquids behave in zero gravity have been flown in the American space shuttle. Curiously the Bristol firm of Christopher Thomas built a tower in the eighteenth century to mould lead shot – an early application of zero gravity effects.*

Bristol. After taking his degree, like many other young physicists, he worked on radar towards the end of the war. He then went on to Harwell, Liverpool University and the European organisation for nuclear research (CERN) at Geneva. In 1960 he was appointed to the Chair of Experimental Physics at Liverpool where he was responsible for the design and building of the Daresbury Laboratory, one of Britain's four 'big science' research facilities. Unusually for a project of this magnitude, the Daresbury Laboratory was finished on time and at the predicted price. Just before he arrived in Bristol Dr Merrison was elected a Fellow of the Royal Society.

His qualities, like those of Sir Philip Morris, were quickly recognised by Government. Despite the continuing uneasy situation for all universities, he was asked to take on the Chairmanship of the Enquiry into Design and Erection of Steel Box Girder Bridges (1970-73); the Committee of Enquiry into the Regulation of the Medical Profession (1972-75); and the Royal Commission on the National Health Service (1976). He became Chairman of the Committee of Vice-Chancellors and Principals, the Chairman of the Advisory Board on the Research Councils, Chairman of the Association of Commonwealth Universities and Chairman of CERN.

But unlike Sir Philip, Dr Merrison did not bring to these posts or to his conduct of the University a personal vision which he wanted to impose on the situation. Instead he brought a hard pragmatic intelligence which sought

in each situation the best practical solution. This in time produced 'Merrison Rules' which now govern both bridge engineering and medical practice; in the University the same method resulted in a shift of emphasis. Where other contemporary Vice-Chancellors sought for their universities deeper relationships with industry or, like Morris, sought to broaden the curriculum on Arnoldian lines, Merrison sought simply the pursuit of excellence. This was a 'neo-Charlottenburg' approach. Universities would justify themselves to government and public not by the immediate relevance of their work or their broad culture but by being superlatively good at their essential task: advancing the frontiers of knowledge and transmitting that knowledge to new generations of scholars in an inspiring way by teaching them what Yeats called "the fascination of what's difficult". Merrison did not thereby reject broader values. He was Chairman of the Bristol Old Vic Theatre Trust and took an active interest in the theatre's affairs and he was also well-known for his catholic taste in reading matter. He saw broader culture as something universities could and should do in extra-curricular ways. Liberal education, as Ashby puts it, should be a spirit of approach, not a choice of subject, or, to put it another way, if Merrison had a philosophy of university life, it was philosophy as Ramsay understood it.

His first concern at Bristol was to get the University's government right. Representatives of students and non-professorial staff were given

Five Glycolytic Enzymes discovered at Bristol. In Biochemistry, Botany and other University departments useful industrial enzymes are continually being discovered.

Helping the Handicapped. The School of Education unit studying sign language (shown here) is only one of a number of University research projects aimed at helping handicapped people. The Brain and Perception Laboratory has produced a device to aid the deaf, the Physics Department has invented a reading machine for the blind and the Department of Electrical and Electronic Engineering ran a joint project with Frenchay Hospital on stroke rehabilitation.

UK6: a satellite designed by the University and built by British Aerospace at Filton.

Balloon launch at Cardington: *the beginning of Bristol's ventures into space.*

membership of the Senate and Council. The presence of the former required Privy Council permission and the Privy Council made it a condition of student membership of such bodies that student representatives should not be present at discussions of the personal affairs (including such matters as promotion etc) of staff and students. In Bristol this led to the creation of a 'reserved area of business' section of the agenda of Senate and Council. When this section was reached student members withdrew from the meeting. Students and non-professorial staff were also admitted to membership of the major committees of these bodies with the exception of the Committee of Deans (Senate) and the Finance Committee (Council). The newly appointed Information Officer was given the right to attend and to report on the meetings of Senate and Council in the new University newspaper, the *Newsletter*.

A few years later the non-academic staff was also given representation on Council. The Council's decision in this matter – that such staff should be directly represented rather than through intermediaries – highlighted a new concern for the University. Since the 1920s academic staff had had a trade union, the Association of University Teachers (AUT). For most of its history, the AUT behaved more like a Friendly Society than a trade union, but in the early 1970s that changed. The AUT joined the Trades Union Congress (interestingly, it was placed in the Entertainment Section) but more importantly the early 1970s also saw the rapid unionisation of other kinds of University employees. The Council had to create Joint Negotiating Committees (JNCs) with the Association of Scientific, Technical and Managerial Staffs (ASTMS [technicians]), the National and Local Government Officers' Association (NALGO [secretarial, clerical and library staff]), and the Transport and General Workers' Union (TGWU [porters, cleaners, gardeners etc]) as well as with the AUT. The JNCs vigorously pursued the implications of legislation such as the Health and Safety at Work Act. New specialist areas of administration such as Personnel and Safety Offices had to be created to deal with the problems identified by a whole new range of University committees.

Occasionally, as in a strike in 1970, trade union problems got confused with the student 'revolutionary' problem. University rates of pay for porters and cleaners were linked to the pay of certain local authority workers. When those workers went on strike, University staff in these grades also felt they had to withdraw their labour. Students tried to exploit the situation but a series of vigorous speeches and actions by the new Vice-Chancellor and a snow-storm of leaflets from the new Information Office reduced the revolutionary ferment, and both the strike and its accompanying student disruption ended without serious damage to relationships in the University.

There were occasional sit-ins for another few years but the University evolved a highly efficient system of legal action, enhanced security of

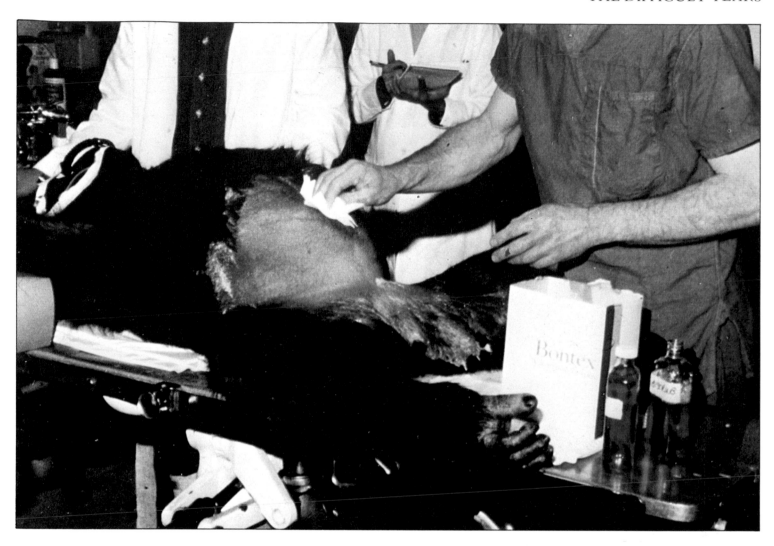

Veterinary School. *From the outset in Medicine, Animal Husbandry and Animal Surgery, the University's Veterinary School has been at the service of the local farming country. University vets have also been called upon to deal with the more exotic animals at the Bristol Zoo. Mother Diana had what is believed to be the first caesarian section carried out on a gorilla. Baby Goliath survived and, after a happy Bristol childhood, now lives in Singapore.*

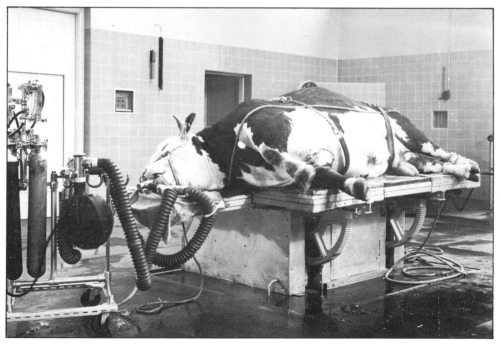

The Tsetse Fly Laboratory. *Sleeping sickness spread by the tsetse fly renders large areas of Africa uninhabitable. Research at Langford into the fly's life-cycle and feeding habits have helped to combat the menace. At first the Langford flies fed on goats but later Bristol developed an artificial membrane (shown here) which gave better scientific control and made the goats redundant. Bristol now exports sterile flies to Africa.*

buildings, better provision of information and more clearly defined student discipline which proved able to reduce both the time taken by, and the effectiveness of, sit-ins. By the end of the decade students were again pursuing their aims through constitutional means and by occasional 'symbolic' and completely non-disruptive occupations of locations agreed in advance with the University authorities.

But even at their most extreme and, notwithstanding the prominence they sometimes achieved in the media, sit-ins never had much effect on the life of the University. As John Cannon pointed out in 1976 "the history of the University even in this period is a story of research and teaching, of labs and lecturers, of music and plays and sport".

One of the great academic developments of 1969 was the University's acceptance of the BEd degree which was to be awarded to students who were taught in the Colleges of Education in Bristol and the surrounding area. This interesting revival of the nineteenth century 'examining university' was the high-water mark of Philip Morris' vision of a graduate teaching profession produced by the universities. The former Department of Education in the Arts Faculty became the Faculty and School of Education. When in 1974, however, a new BEd degree was proposed to replace the existing Certificate of Education as the course of initial training, the University Senate at first refused to sanction the new degree. When it eventually accepted a modified proposal a year later it was too late. The Bristol Colleges had joined the Polytechnic as its Faculty of Education and the other colleges decided to look to the Council for National Academic Awards (CNAA) for their awards (another interesting manifestation of the 'examining university'). The Institute of Education was dissolved. While the University Faculty of Education continued to train teachers in the new more professional BEd, certificate and in-service courses, the dream of an all-graduate teaching profession was left to other non-University academic sources to fulfil. By February 1981 a Senate working party under Professor Ashworth was even suggesting that Education should once again become a department in the Faculty of Arts or alternatively join the Social Sciences Faculty. Another earlier idea, a broader educational curriculum, also received a blow with the demise of the Combined Degree in Arts.

But there were academic initiatives which were successful too. A new School for Advanced Urban Studies (not unlike Geddes' 1920s suggestion in some respects) was founded with Sir Colin Buchanan, the distinguished town planner, as its first director. SAUS later developed its interests in the area of public policy studies in which the University had already established an excellent reputation through the Departments of Social Work and Social Administration (which eventually combined to form the School of Applied Social Studies). Sociology developed interesting research and teaching in ethnic relations and, for a time, the Professor of Sociology, Michael Banton, was also Director of the Social Science Research Council's (SSRC) Research Unit on Ethnic Relations. Social Sciences staff in several departments were seconded to assist national and international government bodies. The Arts Faculty continued in the paths of excellence. In Archaeology, Peter Warren directed important digs at Knossos in Crete while at Salonika an excavation by a Greek professor, Manolis Andronikos, discovered the tomb of Philip of Macedon more or less where Bristol's Professor Hammond had predicted it might be found. In the Sciences, Chemistry and Physics continued to add to their high international reputation. Eglinton, for example, was one of the few British Principal Investigators appointed for the NASA Moon Program and a few years later Haynes was a Principal Investigator on the Spacelab project. The physicists too got into space with UK6 the British satellite and made great strides also in balloon observations of outer space, in glaciology, in material physics and in particle physics. Though the appointment of Mark Richmond as Vice-Chancellor of Manchester was a blow to Bacteriology, it was also a compliment to its high standing. In Medicine, Middlemiss was a world leader in Radiology, and Epstein and Silver in Pathology led distinguished teams to new frontiers in cancer and immunology, and improved microvascular surgery and wound treatments. Butler, in Child Health, virtually invented a major new international centre of childhood studies, based partly on the longitudinal studies he had developed. In

The Dig at Knossos. *This circular dancing floor and evidence of cannibalism were among the unexpected discoveries.*

The Law Faculty *celebrated its Fiftieth Anniversary with an Appeal which it hoped would enable it to build a new purpose-built moot 'court'.*

Announcing the bad news. *One of the* Newsletter *Specials which gave the detailed figures which provided the background to the University's debate on how best to meet the cuts in income.*

Engineering old initiatives grew to fruition. The appointment of Newing in 1930 and Sheppard in 1935 to teach Mathematics to engineers developed in the early 1970s into a new Department of Engineering Mathematics under Milne. Sander and Dagless were appointed to chairs to develop electronics and microelectronics, the science that Bristol Physics under Mott had 'discovered' in the 1930s. Throughout the period the power and size of the University's computer contined to grow.

Bristol staff continued to be sought for chairs in other universities. Horn and Cross, Kirk and Ricks went to Cambridge from Bristol chairs. Randle, with some originality, went to Oxford. Perhaps even more impressively, Bristol staff, like Anderson (Drama) and Bhaskar (Economics) who had not been promoted even to Senior Lecturer, went straight to chairs elsewhere. The Geography Department had an even more extraordinary compliment. Professor Peel, then the Head of Department, received an invitation from an American state university which wished to establish a new centre of excellence in Geography in the USA. The Americans issued an invitation for the entire academic staff of the Department to relocate at their university and at their expense. Although obviously Peel and his colleagues were very flattered, they felt they could not accept and staff in the Department continued to be recruited in the usual way by other universities, going to chairs at Cambridge and elsewhere.

The University's buildings also continued to grow. Twist and Whitley's new University Library, rather uncompromisingly set like a stranded liner at the top of St Michael's Hill, won the support of its users and the admiration of the Library Association which gave it an award. It was studiously ignored by the RIBA who gave an award instead to a rather ugly extension for SAUS at Rodney Lodge. In a limited competition organised in conjunction with the RIBA, the judging panel rejected buildings ranging from something which resembled the National Theatre to a rather pleasant traditional quadrangle and selected an ambitious conservation scheme by Richard MacCormac for a new building for the Arts Faculty. At Langford a clever adaptation of a haybarn became the first good building the University had been able to manage on the site. Perhaps the best scheme was the excellent restoration of Royal Fort House.

To say all this is to say only part of what was going on. To say all that was going on would be to say no more than one would expect of a good university with a national and international reputation in every discipline.

But all this excellence and building was going on against a continuing background of financial problems. In 1973 Mrs Thatcher, the then Minister of Education, announced cuts in university funding. Her reasons were only partly due to a desire to reduce public expenditure. The student revolution, the usual accusations of 'more means worse' levelled at the new universities, the failure of the universities to produce something tangible to show for the investment of the 1960s, combined at Westminster to produce a mood of disenchantment with higher education. In 1974 the incoming Wilson Government shared the Conservatives' lack of regard. Universities, particularly in regard to staff salaries, were made to pay heavily throughout the Labour administration for what some sections of press and Parliament evidently regarded as their past profligate consumption of the nation's wealth in the middle 1960s; in the quaint language of the time, a salary 'anomaly' was followed by a salary 'erosion'. But the seven lean years of cuts failed to alternate with seven years of plenty. The new Conservative Government elected in 1979 was quick to review public expenditure plans. The lead time in such matters is 18 months, and right on time, disaster was foreshadowed in the Budget in March 1981. The shape and scale of the disaster was made clear in letters from the University Grants Committee in July – the universities were in effect to be reduced by 15%.

Bristol received an average cut but other universities like Salford, Bradford, and Aston were very hard hit. In Bristol the Vice-Chancellor worked through August and September with the University's officers to relate the broad sweep of the UGC letter into a recognisable financial answer to the question: what did the cuts mean for Bristol? In October the Senate had a special meeting to receive their report. The message was clear – Bristol faced a stark choice: to reduce all departments by approximately the same amount and become a second-class university by its own standards or to make selective cuts, cutting out some whole areas of study so that what remained would still be strong and good. The Senate chose selective cuts and the Vice-Chancellor, in a display of personal courage, offered to prepare the cuts plan himself. A month later he returned to Senate with his plan. It recommended the closure of Education, Architecture and some small Arts departments (including Russian which had just been singled out for special praise in a UGC report). No department or service in the University was to escape unscathed.

It was hardly to be expected that so radical a plan would be accepted passively, but there was no major confrontation. The plan and the financial background to it were published in special *Newsletters*. Everyone in the University had the facts. In the columns of the *Newsletter* and in both formal and informal meetings the issues were widely discussed.

At Senate Professor Chambers presented an alternative to the Vice-Chancellor's plan in which he broadened the cuts while retaining to some degree the selective principle required by Senate. Senate's discussions were long and complex. Debates were remarkable for their quality – for example, Professor Robinson, Dean of Education, made memorable defences of his Faculty. Eventually a version of the Vice-Chancellor's plan, drawn up by the Deans in the light of successive Senate discussions, was adopted by Senate and Council. Architecture and the Comparative Animal Respiration Unit

The School of Architecture. *Supporters of the School made silent and dignified protests about its closure but the cuts left the University few alternatives.*

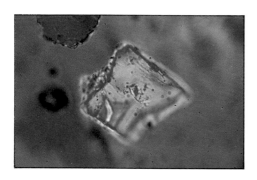

Moon Rock. *A micrograph shows the structure.*

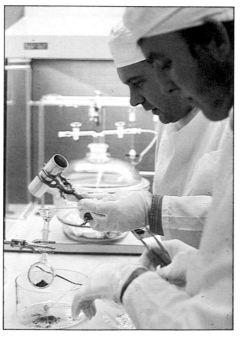

Moon Rock. *Bristol was one of the few world centres to receive American and Russian moon samples.*

were to close, half of Education was to be placed on a self-financing basis, the small Arts departments were to be severely cut and a number of University services were also to have greater than the average University-wide cut which was to be about 10%. The University Court asked for a review of the decision concerning Architecture but a special review committee confirmed the decision.

The 1981 cuts were undoubtedly a terrible blow in Bristol as elsewhere, but the reforms in the University's administration structure enabled them to be carried through in as good a spirit as was possible in the circumstances. The various points were argued fiercely, but there was little acrimony. The blow was softened a little when the Government provided money for a special early retirement and voluntary redundancy fund – in the jargon of Whitehall it was called 'restructuring'. A large number of experienced staff at all levels, some of them in a quite conscious desire to save the careers of younger colleagues, accepted retirement under the scheme. Some agreed to return part-time. The damage done to the nation's research was incalculable and was plain even to the Government. It introduced an annual 'new blood' competition by which it would fund posts for promising young academics. In the first such competition in 1983, Bristol emerged as the leading provincial university with 12 posts. And in the same year the Treasurer of the University was able to confirm that the plan to meet the cuts was on target. By the required date of October 1984, the University would have adjusted to the reduced level of funding and its accounts would be in balance.

Sir Alec Merrison realised that by that date he would have reached his sixtieth birthday and would have served 15 years in the Vice-Chancellorship. He believed that after that date the University would face further problems. He told Council he wished to retire: the end of 'restructuring' would be a good time for another change of leadership.

It is tempting to regard the period 1968-84 as 'the Merrison years' but to do so would not be fair to him or even be accurate. Vice-Chancellors may determine the style of universities by their powers of advocacy or persuasive chairmanship, but a university's history in any given period is beyond the control of any one man, however excellent. Responsibility is too widely spread. The lay members of Council, for example, particularly the Chairman and the Treasurer, play influential roles, and Bristol was fortunate in both offices during this time. Academic progress itself is determined by random factors: the acquisition of funds, a chance discovery, the availability of the right equipment at the right time in the right place. But most of all it depends on the curious human chemistry which is produced by mixing experienced scholars of distinction with new young and enquiring minds. The history of a university therefore is only partly the leadership of great men; but it is essentially the story of its staff and its students.

Chapter Seven

The University's Staff

The academic staff of a university can be memorable for many reasons. Some will be noteworthy because of their scholarship, some because they were excellent teachers and others for some charming eccentricity or accidental circumstances which made them known, loved and remembered by students and colleagues.

The University College of Bristol was incredibly fortunate in its staff. It was, as we have seen, a very poor college; yet it managed to attract very distinguished scholars to its service. The first principal, Marshall, was, in some ways, the founder of his subject but he was awkward with students in a social setting. Ramsay recalled one evening "at Marshall's; a lot of students were there – Marshall looked hopelessly embarrassed, and looked at Mrs Marshall, who was resigned. I tried to open fire, and with the help of one of our men managed to keep things going, but it was slow, slow". Marion Pease, a student at that time, does not remember Mrs Marshall's being so retiring. "Mrs Marshall", she said, "represented the cause of the higher education of women. It is difficult for this generation (*c.* 1920) to realise what that cause meant to us. There were no degree or professional examinations open to women and no college where they could enter on the same terms as men except our own (and possibly one other) – women who wanted to be doctors had to fight their way through incredible difficulties – the High School movement was only just beginning to give women teachers some sort of status and Girton and Newnham only existed on sufferance and got their students examined by the personal kindness of men like Dr Sidgwick and other Fellows of Cambridge colleges". Mildred Loveday said in 1927, "Many of those who were inclined to look with suspicion on a University Education were won over by her combination of youth, mind and beauty".

The Ramsays seem to have found the socialising that the principalship demanded much easier, even though Mrs Ramsay professed shock that the cook demanded "£18 a year wages, besides beer money, we providing sugar and tea" but added "She is an excellent servant and saves her big wages easily". The cook was also hard-working: Mrs Ramsay records one 'grand' dinner: "white soup, fried soles, mutton cutlets, boiled turkey (five shillings)

Mary Paley Marshall – *youth, beauty, intellect.*

Ramsay.

Margaret Buchanan Ramsay: *getting on well with everyone.*

and blancmange". Mrs Ramsay got on well with everyone – even the formidable Jowett whom she called 'Uncle Jowett'. Ramsay, like Marshall before him, became known as 'one of Jowett's young men' – a tribute to his personal qualities and his scholarship.

Ramsay was a superb leader and no circumstance affecting the College escaped him. He recorded in letters to his father a loan of £30 to Henry, his lab boy. The boy's father was in the hands of the money lenders but it evidently worked out all right. Henry remained in Ramsay's service and his brother was given a job in the College office.

Ramsay established a small research school, and it was said that he suggested to one of his students, Miss Katherine Williams, that she might like to try to repeat Cavendish's experiment on air. Miss Williams, who had been working on the chemistry of cooked fish, chose instead the determination of the oxygen dissolved in water. She missed a great opportunity: it was the attempt to repeat Cavendish's experiment that, at University College, London, led Ramsay and his collaborators to the discovery of neon, helium and the other inert gases which brought him world fame.

Ramsay became famous because he was, although a brilliant lecturer and an able administrator, primarily an investigator. There were others on the academic staff, however, who were (or became famous later because they were) excellent teachers. James Rowley, Professor of Modern History and Literature, was one such. Canon Gamble recalled that his students "went away from his lectures feeling that he had opened up to us sources of joy, springs of life to which we should have access, no matter what our future life might be, whether we became rich or poor, solitary or surrounded with friends". George Hare Leonard claimed that, as a result of Rowley's lectures, he tended to hear passages of literature "in what it must be confessed was a very imitable – and indeed constantly imitated – Irish tongue". If the imitators were accurate this was no mean achievement. Rowley came to Bristol from Dungannon where the local accent has strange survivals of Elizabethan pronunciation overlying the basic Northern Irish accent. Morris Travers knew Rowley personally and was not easily impressed. He was prepared to recognise Rowley as a genuine scholar and to suggest that he was passed over twice for the Principalship because it was recognised his talents were scholarly rather than administrative.

Another excellent teacher who in fact was an excellent administrator was Silvanus Thompson. A Quaker, Thompson was appointed first as lecturer but was raised to the Chair of Physics. While he was adept at devising his own apparatus – in so poor a College he had to be – he was more a teacher than an investigator. He thought deeply about teaching and was the author of several textbooks on calculus, electricity, and magnetism which went

Musical evening. *At home with the Silvanus Thompson family.*

through over 40 editions. He was also the author of the standard biographies of Faraday and Kelvin. He was one of the first people to advocate *technical* education. He came to this view through his extensive travels on the Continent. Like Ramsay, he was impressed by the German system. (One may note here that all these scientists were fluent in three or four European languages. Thompson could and did lecture in Italian and Ramsay claimed he owed his Bristol appointment to his fluent Dutch. Thompson was not only a physicist and electrical engineer, he was also accomplished in music and painting. There was no problem about 'the two cultures' then.) Unlike Ramsay, he did not see the need to achieve a British Charlottenburg. He wanted to establish a system of lower level technical education and he was among the first to suggest that, since it would be a state responsibility, there should be a Minister of Education in the Government. Thompson left Bristol in 1885 to become Principal of Finsbury Technical College where he remained for the next 30 years. He continued his interest in technical education and became in 1899 President of the Institution of Electrical Engineers. The national reputation he has left behind is one of great distinction, sufficient, for example, to warrant a brief biography published by the Science Museum in 1979. His Bristol reputation is more personal and endearing. Many recalled his appearance when the British Association met in Bristol. Thompson attended wearing a different coloured cravat each day,

Silvanus   Thompson,   artist.   An accomplished study, typical of his work.

the colours being those of the spectrum. As Ramsay remarked, Silvanus' colleagues could not decide whether the effect was *silly* or *vain*.

Professor Ryan's propensity to this sort of word-play has been noted earlier. Practical jokes were also characteristic of the time. Professor Sollas, who left the University College for Dublin and afterwards went to a chair in Oxford, has had his name persistently associated with one. It is alleged that he invented the famous 'Piltdown Man' but that the whole affair grew so quickly he was not able to acknowledge it. Geologists now place little credence in the story of Sollas' involvement, and the only man who might have known for certain, Dr Turner, for many years Warden of Mortimer House Hall of Residence and one of Sollas' last students, died without revealing the reason for his enigmatic smiles when the matter was raised. There was perhaps confirmation of a kind which was revealed only after the death of Professor J. A. Douglas. Douglas, another of Sollas' last students, left a tape-recording about the Piltdown affair which was published posthumously in *Nature* and which clearly indicated that it was a hoax and that Sollas was involved.

Such frivolity would not have pleased May Staveley. She succeeded Miss Rosamund Earle and Miss Tuke (later Dame Margaret and Principal of Bedford College, London) as Tutor for Women Students and played a leading role in the purchase of Clifton Hill House as the University's first hall of residence. She was not a scholar, and her students recalled her teaching as 'conscientious but not inspiring'. (The inspiration in the History Department came from George Hare Leonard, a colourful figure in brown and green homespun clothes made by Somerset weavers.) Yet Miss Staveley was loved by her students. She expected a high standard of work and behaviour. Every student had to shake hands with her at breakfast in the morning – a daunting prospect for the late-comer – but she lavished great care and generosity on them. No one ever came to her with a problem in vain. Students remember such things with gratitude as they remember with affection her succession of Pekingese dogs and her dreadful cockatoo.

A few years earlier another staff pet, a fox terrier called Tony, belonging to Lloyd Morgan, made an interesting contribution to science. All modern animal psychology has grown from the work of Lloyd Morgan in England and the early work of E. L. Thorndike in America. Lloyd Morgan established a tradition of careful observation of behaviour in natural settings. He had observed Tony learn to carry a stick with a heavy knob on one end and to open a gate by putting his head under the latch. To describe this Lloyd Morgan introduced the term 'trial and error learning'. One of the best subsequent experiments on the strengthening of responses by reward was done by a pupil of Lloyd Morgan, Grindley, after he had left Bristol and gone to Cambridge.

Conwy Lloyd Morgan: *without a beard*

and developing his image.

Miss Staveley: *with parrot and dogs.*

Professor Skemp. *A rare civilian picture.*

The careers of Lloyd Morgan and Miss Staveley in Bristol span the period when the University was founded. In this period there was a number of distinguished scholars who also had a profound social influence. In particular there was a small group called the Men's Lecture Committee (which despite its name was really a forerunner of the AUT) which included in its number Ferrier (Engineering), McBain and Francis Francis. According to Tyndall, it is difficult to over-emphasise the contribution this group made to the developing University. It founded, or caused others to found, the Students' Union, the AUT, the University Diary, the University newspaper *Nonesuch* (the first editor was a History lecturer, E. A. Walker), the OTC, the Alumni Association and the Athletics Ground. Some of these, like the OTC, were Bristol versions of national movements. The OTC nationally was 'invented' by Haldane: his Bristol adherents produced one of the leading contingents, possibly due to the energy of Skemp and McBain. During the war Skemp, who had been the successful candidate when Cowl's English Chair was advertised, proved himself to be as excellent at teaching military matters as he had been in the field of Literature. To his considerable embarrassment, although his students confessed they would like nothing better than 'to go over the top with Skemp', the War Office valued his training capabilities so highly they would not allow him to go to the Front. In the end he managed to wangle it by dropping in rank to Lieutenant. He acquitted himself with gallantry but was tragically killed only ten days before the war ended. His colleague and comrade-in-arms Capitaine Félix Boillot wrote in the *Nonesuch,* "J'admirais entre autres dons cet éclectisme de goûts, cette large et tolérante sympathie intellectuelle pour toutes les nouvelles idées, tous les efforts sincères et j'ai toujours pensé que c'était là une des vraies causes de ses succès de professeur. Son imagination complaisante et féconde lui faisait en effet sentir d'instinct les besoins de ses étudiants – il se recréait pour ainsi dire à leur mesure et faisait toute la route avec eux.

"Il avait leur confiance comme il avait leur admiration. Tous et toutes allaient lui soumettre leurs embarras, leur incertitudes, aussi heureux de recourir à cette obligeance qu'il l'était lui-même de les servir. Car il aimait à se rendre utile: je sais de lui maint trait qui le prouve et qui montrerait de quelle délicatesse se paraît cette obligeance."

The *Nonesuch* magazine also described McBain, "He possesses, to an extraordinary degree, the personal magnetism which can fill others with a sense of power, and with a feeling that difficulties at first sight appalling, will inevitably be overcome". Other members of the Committee achieved distinction. Francis Francis of course became Acting Vice-Chancellor.

The staff who joined the new University from the Merchant Venturers' Technical College were less remarkable in their own subjects and in their personalities, but J. W. Burrough, who began his studies at the MVTC in 1904 remembered Darnall-Smith (Chemistry), who lost all his research records in the 1906 fire, and Boulton (Mathematics) and Munro (Engineering) with gratitude. He also remembered Julius Wertheimer with affection but, perhaps because of the animosity aroused at the time of the University campaign, the anecdotes which have come down to us about Wertheimer are not all favourable.

As permanent Dean of the Faculty *and* Principal of the MVTC Wertheimer ran a régime of iron. When one of the staff, a lecturer called Baker whose salary was £160 p.a. (when Wertheimer's was £1,100), pointed out that he was on the borderline for compulsory insurance contributions, Wertheimer agreed that the situation was unfortunate. Clearly Baker's salary would need to be raised to obviate the difficulty. In those days lecturers were paid by the term in December, April and July. Baker waited. When his next salary cheque arrived Baker found that Wertheimer had kept his promise. His salary had been raised to one hundred and sixty pounds – and one shilling. Baker was disappointed but there were others who thought that the settlement was generous by Wertheimer's standards. It could have been one penny.

Happily for the University, Wertheimer was succeeded as Permanent Dean of Engineering and Principal of the College by Andrew Robertson. In the opinion of J. L. M. Morrison, only Tyndall rivalled Robertson in his benign influence in the University in the period 1919-1949. Morrison's view is confirmed by Shepherd, who joined the University in 1935. In Shepherd's opinion Robertson had a genius for personal relationships. He was apparently the kind of man who could call someone a 'bloody fool' without giving offence. In fact, the person so described very often agreed with the description when Robertson explained the reasons for his remark in what he called 'a moment of prayer' – a discreet interview in which only he and the recipient of his rebuke were present. Robertson's vitality was as remarkable as his tact. Even when he was well into his eighties he persisted in bounding up the steps of the Wills Memorial Building, exciting admiration and concern in almost equal measure among his younger colleagues.

Tyndall was remarkable throughout his long career as student, lecturer and professor in the University, for his personal kindliness and his ability to spot and develop talent. As an investigator himself he was perhaps not in the first rank of physicists but he was a very able administrator and saw that other people, perhaps more talented than he in that direction, got the wherewithal to develop their work. He was an excellent teacher and enjoyed in full measure that rather rare gift among university teachers – the ability to see when a promising young researcher would benefit more by someone else's guidance. Apart from his contribution to the science side of the University, Tyndall was also extremely influential in helping to establish the Drama Department and perhaps was of vital importance in establishing the Chair of Music. He waited until he was conducting his last Senate as Acting

Andrew Robertson.

The University 1925 – *all of it.*

Vice-Chancellor before suggesting, under 'Any other business', that the University should establish a Chair in Music. He was also influential in helping his successor as Vice-Chancellor, Philip Morris, to select W. K. Stanton as the first incumbent. Music and Drama were both fortunate in the quality of the scholars they attracted to their first Chairs.

Another outstanding personality of the earlier part of that period was O. C. M. Davis. Honoured by the Government during the war for work on respirators, Davis was a scientist, a qualified doctor and a qualified lawyer, and practised all three professions. Travers remarks that he always sent students in need of medical attention to Davis "because the Clifton doctors are no good". He had personal reasons for such confidence. He attributed the recovery of his seriously-ill grandson to Davis: under other care the child was manifestly dying.

Travers had returned to Bristol in 1927 after sojourns in India and America. He was appointed first as a Fellow and then as Honorary Professor. Francis Francis wrote before he arrived expressing the hope "that we will make the old place hum". Unfortunately, soon after Travers' arrival both his professorial colleagues, Francis and Garner, fell ill and he had to take on the unexpected burden of administering the School of Chemistry. Travers recorded that he found this difficult in a place where, as he put it, "the whole administration is of the comic opera order". Travers also recorded the curious information that Bristol at this date had no Senior Common Room. Loveday for some reason was opposed to the idea and the SCR did not appear until after the Second World War when Sir Philip Morris was very much in favour.

Travers' second period in Bristol was not as productive as his first and his scientific work on infra-red problems, though interesting in identifying a productive line of enquiry, did not result in papers of the major kind published jointly with Ramsay 30 years earlier. The major scientific work in Bristol in the 1930s was in the Physics Department, where at one time no less than three future Nobel Laureates were working. They were Mott, Powell and Bethe. A fourth Nobel Laureate, Dirac, had already left for Cambridge. (Dirac was educated at the Merchant Venturers' School and graduated in Engineering in 1921. He left Bristol in 1923 after spending two years in the study of mathematics and took his PhD at Cambridge in 1925. His theories marked the start of the investigation into anti-particles and anti-matter.)

The Department was headed by Nevill Mott. Mott himself saw his time in Bristol as being significant in that Bristol was the first major centre to recognise the importance of the German physicist R. N. Pohl and his ideas about what is now called 'solid state physics'. Bristol was the first university to call an international conference to discuss the matter. But although Mott received his Nobel Prize for fundamental investigation of the electronic structure of magnetic and disordered systems, he is remarkable among physicists in that he developed the theoretical base in several areas of physics, including particle physics and materials science. For Mott the step from mathematical or theoretical physics to the understanding of real materials was a short one.

Mott was remarkable not only as an investigator but as a teacher. Bernard Lovell was one student who remembered the vitality and liveliness of his lectures. Mott was remarkably young (28) when appointed and when he left in 1954 to succeed W. L. Bragg at the Cavendish Laboratory in Cambridge he had many productive years of physics ahead of him. His able administration and leadership created at the Wills Laboratory a spendid team which has continued the high reputation for Bristol physics which he created.

The work of the second Nobel Laureate, although he stayed in Bristol for only a short time, was peculiarly appropriate to the laboratory. The building is decorated externally with the badge of the Wills family, the sun in splendour, and Hans Bethe is most widely known for his theory of how the Sun obtains and radiates its energy. Born in Strasbourg, in 1933 he was dismissed by the Nazis from his assistant professorship at Tübingen because his mother was Jewish. While at Bristol he wrote a number of important papers on nuclear physics and on radiation theory, including one with another refugee, Heitler, on electron-positron production.

Arthur Mannering Tyndall.

Paul Dirac *with his mother before receiving his Nobel Prize.*

Cecil Powell speaking after receiving his *Nobel Prize.*

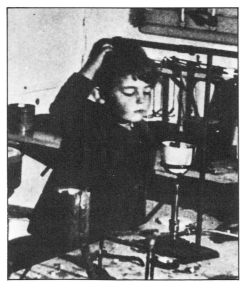

Starting young. Professor Peter Fowler *as a boy in the lab opened by his grandfather, Lord Rutherford, in which he was to become Royal Society Professor.*

The third Nobel Laureate was Cecil Powell. When he arrived in Bristol in 1927 he was only 24, a recent PhD of Cambridge. Bristol had been interested in photographic materials for many years. Between 1935-45 Powell developed techniques for using photographic emulsion to detect, by their tracks, individual nuclear particles and to study low-energy nuclear reactions. His low-cost techniques proved to be at least the equal of other more expensive ways of investigation.

By 1947 he was using his emulsions to study cosmic rays by sending them aloft in huge balloons launched from the University playing fields. The results were exciting for physicists everywhere but exasperating for British Railways when one balloon landed in the path of a Bristol to Bath express. In later years the balloons, the hunt for particles and the exasperation of transport officials, were extended first to Italy and then to the United States. Powell's discovery of the pion (pi-meson) in 1947 made him the father of modern particle physics.

But Powell was important in other ways. He, like Mott, was an inspiring teacher and research leader. He also was not just a physicist. Like Mott, he became concerned about where their research was leading and became a leader in the movement to discuss, and raise awareness about, the social responsibilities of science. He took a leading part in the world conference on science at Pugwash in Nova Scotia in 1957. The richness and variety of his work drew a tribute which would certainly have pleased the Wills, who built his laboratory. Speaking at the 1953 Rochester Conference, Leprince Ringuet, of the École Polytechnique, said, in Europe "Bristol est le soleil".

The Nobel Laureates were not, of course, the only major figures in Physics, nor in the University. Skinner, for example, was doing distinguished work and it was he who, with Cockcroft (Cambridge), Chadwick (Liverpool), Oliphant (Birmingham), and Massey (London), clarified ideas on what became Harwell at a war-time meeting in Washington. As Sanderson has noted, whereas the First World War was won by the chemists, the Second World War was won by the physicists. The strength of Bristol physics in the 1930s and the contribution it made to the war played a major role in establishing Bristol as an important centre in the eyes not only of other scientists but in the corridors of power in Westminster and elsewhere.

There were distinctions in other departments too. In Medicine the leading figures were Bruce Perry and Tom Hewer. Hewer started the widely emulated Bristol Bone Tumour Registry and Perry, apart from his contributions to Cardiac Medicine, also started a Students' Health Service, only the third of its kind in the country. Both possessed the love of gardens and gardening which characterised many of Bristol's leading figures of the 1930s. Hewer, although by profession a pathologist, was appointed an official collector of some specimens by Kew Gardens, and he and Bruce

Perry made good use of journeys undertaken as external examiners. Hewer's garden at Vine House, Henbury, was in later years open to the public and Bruce Perry's garden at Coombe Dingle, especially in his retirement, became the scene of many pleasant informal University gatherings.

One of the leading figures on the Arts side of the University from the 1930s was the blind Canadian C. M. McInnes, known universally as 'Mac'. The name of his subject, Imperial History, rings strangely in modern ears but at that time, when independence for India was the only item on the de-colonisation agenda and the Imperial Conference at Westminster had just been held, it seemed central to the subject. The strong interest McInnes established was continued with appropriate changes of emphasis in later years by Kenneth Ingham and, today, Bristol is one of the few universities with a long tradition in the study of African history. But 'Mac's' influence was not confined to the lecture room. He had a great social influence. For example, he founded a dining club called the '36 Club'. The idea was that staff members should invite a student guest for a meal after which they should hear a speech on some topic of moment or interest by a distinguished speaker. From the outset it was an all-male affair and it was not until the early 1970s that anyone had the temerity to invite a female student – even then the case was special. The member was the Vice-Chancellor and his guest the President of the Union. When 'Mac' died the Club changed its name to the "MacInnes Club" in his memory.

Of course it is possible that McInnes was right to maintain his club as an all-male affair. Some of the women members of staff were truly formidable. Miss Shapland, for example, had begun her career in the University as Isambard Owen's secretary soon after the granting of the Charter. In 1928 she became the first Secretary of the University and three years later succeeded E. G. Francis as Registrar. She seems to have terrified almost everyone who worked with her but it was under her direction that the foundations of the present University Administration were laid. Dr Millicent Taylor was impressive in other ways. She worked hard in her subject, Chemistry, and was dearly loved by her students. Her prowess as a mountaineer was legendary. During the war years she taught students how to climb with ropes so that they could if necessary escape from, or get to the seat of, fires started by enemy action. And after the war tradition claims that, as the University's first Accommodation Officer, she personally investigated all the routes by which young agile students might gain entrance to halls after the doors were locked (a necessary skill at a time when women students were allowed only a few late passes a session). Since Dr Taylor was over 60 at the time this was no mean feat.

In the Arts Faculty the major scholarly figure of the post-war years undoubtedly was Kitto. When Kitto was appointed to the Chair of Greek from a lectureship in Glasgow in 1944, William Beare held the Chair of

"Mac", a bust by Epstein.

Dr Allan Rogers, *for many years the bearer of the University's Mace, was a member of the British Transarctic Expedition of 1956-58.*

Latin. Kitto's great scholarly work was *Greek Tragedy,* Beare's was *The Roman Stage.* The Winterstoke Professor of English was D. G. James (later Vice-Chancellor of Southampton), who also was interested in drama. These three not only created the Department of Drama but created the approach to the literature of other nations and other times through plays in performance. Kitto, for example, tested his translations of *Antigone* and *Electra* in departmental productions for which he also wrote the music. He achieved a deserved popular reputation through his best-selling Pelican *The Greeks.* But he was a man on whom his scholarship sat lightly. He took the Greeks seriously but little else. He enjoyed music and had considerable expertise in extemporising verse. On one occasion he delighted children at tea with some nonsense reminiscent of Carroll or Lear:

> *"Strange to think the infant Livy*
> *Never tasted Cheller's jivy,*
> *Nor stretched out an eager paw*
> *Towards a dish of stramberry jaw."*

His farewell speech in the University at his retirement party was typical of him. This distinguished scholar, full of years and wisdom, ended his remarks by recalling his Gloucestershire boyhood. He told a tale of storms on the river and how, after one such storm, he had encountered a bargeman whose barge had broken free and was drifting down the river. What moral was he to draw from this, his audience wondered. Kitto concluded with the bargeman's remark, "The bogger's gawn". And sat down. It was a fitting self-deprecating jest with which to end 20 years in which he had advanced his own subject and drama, taught vividly and made friends easily.

Kitto was perhaps the last professor to be known widely throughout the University for his scholarship and his personality, although the performances directed by W. K. Stanton and his successors in the Chair of Music and Glynne Wickham and colleagues in the Drama Department brought great delight. The intimate scale of the University in the 1940s and 1950s permitted everyone to know staff in other departments but as the explosion of student numbers and staff numbers progressed in the 1960s, it became less and less possible for people to be known and to be appreciated outside their own or cognate disciplines. Hinton in Zoology, for example, was a delightful man. A world authority on insects, academically and institutionally he did not suffer fools gladly. He expressed himself trenchantly and outside his department may have been regarded as a difficult colleague. But those who knew him knew his delight in jokes of all kinds, particularly practical ones. For example, on an expedition in Mexico it fell to him to shoot ducks to supplement the rations. He had taken a dislike to one member of the expedition whose commentary on events had outrun his knowledge of them. Hinton determined to put him in his place. Realizing that one roasted fowl looks very much like another, Hinton saw to it that everyone had a succulent

Support staff. *(left to right): Don Boulton, Dan Scully, Pat Sheehan, Ken Boulton, Charlie Whitrow.*

duck except the offender whose meal was peculiarly difficult to eat. For him, Hinton had shot and roasted a seagull. Such treatment was for those he considered fools. His students and colleagues always had his unfailing and generous support.

Likeable and well-known characters were not, of course, confined to the academic staff. Generations of Bristol students remember with affection other staff such as Dan Scully, who served the University for over 50 years. He was born in Frogmore Street at the bottom of the hill on which the University stands. He was educated at a little school in the area and started working for the University in the Wills Memorial Building soon after it opened. He ended his career as Head Porter at the top of the hill in Senate House. Only in retirement did he go 'abroad' – across the Clifton Suspension Bridge to Bracken Hill. When Dan Scully retired he was succeeded by Pat Sheehan who also served the University for 50 years. Leonard Bullock and Fred Moore, who both worked in the Finance Office, Edward Seavill of Geology, Harold Freke of Geography, and Edward Livingstone of Zoology also achieved their half-century. The University has had a way of attracting longevity of service. Alfred Davis, the Examinations Officer, and his successor, Bob Harrison, both served only a few months short of 50 years and their length of service was almost matched by Bert Attwell, a groundsman at Coombe Dingle. The Boulton family – a father and two sons

The Duke of Beaufort. *The University's fourth Chancellor quite literally at home with his dogs.*

– had over a hundred years of service among them and Bill Stevens, the 'theatrical impresario' of the Victoria Rooms was another long-term servant of the University. And there are certainly others whose fame and importance goes beyond their departments – men such as Kevin Tindall in Physics, (it is curious how people of that surname are drawn to the area at the top of St Michael's Hill) who first arrived at Bristol to do war-work in the University while serving in the Navy.

But the staff are not the only memorable people in the University. Throughout its history the high office of Chancellor seems to have been curiously symbolic of the University. The duties of the post are ceremonial and Chancellors are rarely seen in the University except on formal occasions, but their presence on particular occasions often has typified the spirit of the University. When Churchill was appointed to succeed Haldane, for example, he was a major Conservative figure and a recent Chancellor of the Exchequer (the University kept a political balance by giving Snowden, the Labour Chancellor of the Exchequer, an Honorary Degree). But at the time of his appointment he was unpopular in his own party and his political career seemed at an end. Loveday sought the advice of the Chairman of the UGC, Sir William McCormick. McCormick, a Highlander, must have been genuinely blessed with second sight that Scotsmen of his origins sometimes claim. He predicted future great fame for Churchill as Prime Minister. John Buchan, another Scot consulted by Loveday, concurred in this judgement. If Churchill had died in the 1930s when he was on the back benches of Parliament, he would have gone down in the nation's history as a failed politician and in the University's history as a Chancellor whose term of office had no particular significance. The war which brought Churchill to the premiership, by accident brought him to Bristol at a peculiarly appropriate time. Bristol had just endured one of the most damaging enemy air-raids. Much of the city and several parts of the University had been destroyed. Churchill came to award honorary degrees to the American Ambassador and the Australian Prime Minister. The degrees were conferred in the Wills Memorial Building where the Great Hall had been destroyed. Churchill used the occasion both at the time and in later speeches in the USA to affirm his defiance of the enemy, his gratitude to the Allies, and his belief in all the civilised values the University and the nation stood for. Apart from his words, the presence of the Prime Minister in the bomb-damaged University in the middle of a still-smouldering city did much to symbolize the unity everyone felt at the time.

Churchill was succeeded by the Duke of Beaufort. For the University at large it was an appropriate appointment for his was one of "the founding families". For some radical students he and his office were outdated anachronisms, but the way even the recalcitrant revolutionaries returned from a visit to the Chancellor's home at Badminton, won over by his charm

and dignity to the aristocracy and even the hereditary principle, was symbolic of the abiding quality of decent civilized values.

Later in much less dramatic and in some ways more parochial circumstances, another Chancellor seemed to symbolize the University. She was Dorothy Hodgkin, the first non-royal woman to serve in such an office in a British university. In 1976 in a special degree ceremony to mark the centenary of the founding of University College, Bristol, Professor Hodgkin conferred an Honorary Degree upon the American Ambassador, Anne Armstrong (the first woman to hold such a post in a major country). It was an event which was not only appropriate in itself but which symbolized all that the founders had hoped for. Had Bishop Percival, Benjamin Jowett and those who supported them, been told that in 100 years a Quaker woman, a Nobel Laureate, who held a Chair at Oxford, who was the academic tutor of Britain's first woman Prime Minister, and who was titular head of their University grown to international standing, should honour, by conferring a degree upon her, a woman who was an outstanding politician and academic in American life, they would have wished for no more as they opened the doors of their infant college to the first students in 1876.

Dorothy Hodgkin. *The University's fifth Chancellor honours America's first woman Ambassador to the Court of St James.*

The Chancellor *in the more informal role she loves – talking to University children at the Founders' Day fête.*

Chapter Eight

The Students

The premises which greeted the first students when they turned up for the first classes in October 1876 were not impressive. The two Georgian houses at 32 Park Row, rented by the College Council, were always intended to be temporary. Park Row at that time was a mixture of residential property and shops. Its most notable structure was the New Theatre Royal (afterwards called the Prince's Theatre) which had opened in 1867. The northern side of the road (where Woodland Road now runs) was open grassland and trees, the lower part of the park owned by the Tyndalls of Royal Fort House. The attraction of these premises for the College was their location. Park Row was the border of 'old Bristol'; to the north, beyond Tyndall's Park, there were rapidly burgeoning suburbs of Cotham, Redland and Clifton, the districts from which the College Council expected their women students to come; to the south, lay the industrial and commercial districts whose young men the Council hoped to attract.

The infant College offered day classes and evening classes. In the day classes women outnumbered men (69 to 30) and in the evenings men outnumbered women (143 to 95). The minimum age for admission was 16 years, but in the evening classes there were some very much older students. Marshall recalled, "Three-fourths of those attending day classes are between the ages of 18 and 22; and probably rather more than half of those attending the evening classes are of that age; but many of those attending the evening classes are well advanced in years. In my own class I have two men with grey hairs".

"The women who attend the day classes are chiefly the daughters of the best families in the town. The male students come from nearly the same classes, but not quite, because the tendency is for the sons of the richest inhabitants still to go to Oxford or Cambridge."

The individual quality of the first students was often high. Mrs Marshall recalled "relays of Frys, Peases, Sturges and others of like calibre". Marion Pease, later Mistress of Method in the Day Training College, was there on the first morning. She had walked across Durdham Down with her friend and fellow student Amy Bell, who was one of the first three scholarship

holders. An Indian Mutiny orphan, Amy lived at Cook's Folly, then the only house overlooking the Avon Gorge. She met Marion at the White Tree and they walked together to the bottom of Blackboy Hill, where they took one of the new trams introduced by George White in 1874, to the top of Park Street. In the winter months, this can't have been a pleasant journey – the gas lamps stopped at the White Tree but it appears to have been character-forming. Amy Bell went on to become the first woman stockbroker. Unable to gain admission to the Exchange because she was a woman, she operated through a friendly firm and made a great success.

After their bleak journey students found little comfort. The doors were opened by Charles White the porter (who has the double distinction of being the first non-academic staff employee and the first person to make a phone call in Bristol: he rang Principal Marshall to ask on which board to place a notice).

The students then proceeded to a small cloak-room. Marion Pease remembers that "It was furnished with three or four wooden chairs and a small deal table and with pegs for our heavy cloth waterproofs (mackintoshes had not then been invented). Imagine how stuffy it was on a wet day. Here we worked and ate the lunch we had brought with us and here, in spite of the surroundings, I think I spent some of the happiest hours of my life – with new friends and those talks which at 18 seem so exciting". There were limits

A Pride of Sturges. The Sturge family was prominent in Non-Conformist circles in Bristol. They lived in a house which is now the home of the Theology Department. They not only helped to found the University College, but all the sons and daughters went there as students.

101

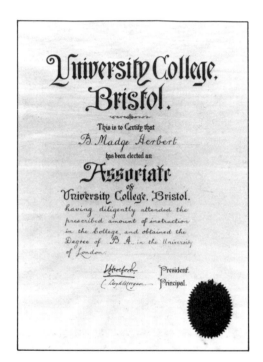

UCB Certificate. *The University College awarded certificates. If a student wanted a degree, application had to be made to the University of London examiners.*

Henry Hele Shaw.

to the excitement. The women's debating society started by Mrs Marshall became so lively on one occasion that the meeting had to be adjourned (the topic was Irish Home Rule) and Marion Pease recalled "a group of us, greatly daring, walked up Park Row to sign a petition which was taking signatures outside the Museum (the present Refectory) for some reform, and we planned a paper chase – there were no athletics of course – which fell through under the disapprobation of Clifton parents".

Relations between the sexes were distant and formal. Miss Pease and her fellow women students were carefully chaperoned in the Victorian manner – even when they went to London for degree examinations they had to have a chaperone on the train and in some cases in the examination hall itself. Miss Pease records a number of details about a fellow student – a student of engineering, Henry Hele Shaw. He lodged with the sister of one of the Pease family servants. One senses a blighted romance. Miss Pease remained at Bristol and Hele Shaw became successively a research assistant, a lecturer, and a professor at Bristol before going on to a chair at Liverpool and a career of great distinction.

The opportunities for students of the opposite sex to meet were scarce. College clubs and societies were few. Chattock in the 1890s spoke of founding clubs and societies "for the cultivation of brain and muscle" and there were spasmodic attempts to keep going athletic teams for cricket, rugby and association football. According to Professor Reynolds (1894), staff members played in these teams and later in hockey and lawn tennis teams. Marshall believed that sport should afford at least the chance of breaking a limb. A student called Fawcett who captained the cricket team had a narrow escape in non-sporting circumstances. He was a research student and during a storm a decorative griffin on the college building fell on him. He survived.

Student entertainments were the entertainments of the typical Victorian home. Mrs Barrell, wife of the Professor of Mathematics, recalled "constant musical evenings, games and whist parties" arranged for student entertainment in the houses of staff. Book teas and quotation parties were also popular. (The Marshalls, the Ramsays, the Lloyd Morgans and the Barrells all had student lodgers.) Ramsay, G. H. Leonard reported, "practised the rarely cultivated art of parlour whistling". When the new college buildings in University Road became available there was some attempt to create a social focus for the women students. A women's Reading Room was established. Mrs Barrell remembered it as "a comfortable pleasant room with pictures of celebrated women hung upon the walls". Mrs Barrell recalled that Elizabeth Barrett Browning was particularly attractive and a student of the time remembered Florence Nightingale in a suitably inspirational pose. In 1899 Miss Rosamund Earle, a distinguished member of Newnham College, Cambridge, who had been appointed "to promote social intercourse among the women students and to care for them as their tutor",

started the Women's Guild. The name suggests an early attempt at a students' union: in practice it was a way of organising social work among the poor and needy (what today's students call social or community action). The debates initiated by Mrs Marshall were continued by the Women's Literary Society under the chairmanship of Mrs Lloyd Morgan. Her husband was also active in entertaining the students. He contributed songs to entertainments given by the musical students of the Day Training College.

One popular form of entertainment was the 'conversazione' when the various laboratories would be open and demonstrations would be given by students of some recent discovery or object of interest. When liquid air was in its early stages, its effect on various objects – such as strawberries – drew many visitors. Other favourite activities were reading parties in rural places outside Bristol and geological expeditions by horse-drawn charabancs to Stanton Drew and Weston.

Outside these academically-linked activities nothing very much of an organised kind seems to have been done for the men students. They could play racquets against the wall of the Rifle Drill Hall and they too had a room at the College but, if one is to believe the *Times and Mirror* of 2 March 1905, it was not used to the best advantage. "It is not going too far to say", thundered this prestigious local paper, "that, unless the misuse of the students' room is soon put a stop to, the Bristol Medical School will be

The Women's Guild *was the first organised attempt to do social work. Miss Herbert, a student around 1908, remembers taking soup with another girl student to the poor around St James Barton. Later houses in Ducie Road were purchased and a University Settlement along the lines pioneered by Toynbee Hall in London was established. George Oatley gave his services free and a centre with a resident warden (for much of the time Hilda Cashmore) was established at Barton Hill. It was so successful that daughter settlements were set up at places such as Hartcliffe and Shirehampton. These early opportunities for involvement with social work in time grew into a formal commitment by the University to train social workers and eventually in very recent years to the formation of a School of Applied Social Studies. The old University paternalism gave way to self-governing community associations. Only the original Barton Hill settlement still bears the name 'University Settlement'. Ironically the Settlement buildings are almost all that is left of old Barton Hill. A combination of enemy action and post-war planning destroyed the old rows of small slum houses. Modern Barton Hill is high-rise flats set in open grasslands but these too have their problems and the Community Association premises are in constant use.*

ruined". The evil deed which provoked the outburst was the excessive playing of *bridge*. Other male students frequented a billiard room and a café in the Triangle.

Student life in the University College, it seems, had little corporate existence. Student clubs and societies seem to have led a fitful life and only those associated with subjects, like the Physical Society or the Engineering Society, had a continuing existence.

The Medical students had their own Union, and a successful dramatic society (founded in 1878 and mainly producing Robertson, Pinero and other Victorian favourites). They also had a magazine called *The Stethoscope*. There was a Students Representative Council with separate membership for men and women but it was not well supported. Its discussions revolved around such matters as the proper manner to record their satisfaction at the Principal's safe return from a conference in America.

This low level of corporate awareness contrasts sharply with the situation in Ireland and in Scotland, where well organised students' unions of a recognisably modern type had their own club buildings and, in the case of Belfast, were making strong and successful representations to the Government for student membership of university governing bodies. Unions of this kind, according to Mackay, Muir, Haldane and the other Scots theorists of British universities, were needed in the emerging provincial English universities. Their Bristol adherents, McBain in particular, saw the creation of a student union as an essential part of their scheme to found a university. In 1906 McBain and his colleagues on the Men's Lectures Committee set about creating one.

A meeting was called in a room above a shop in Queen's Road. Few students attended but the Union was formed. A joint meeting with the Medical Students' Union chaired by Professor Walker-Hall brought the amalgamation of the two unions. Ferrier brought the Engineering Society into membership shortly afterwards. A proposal to bring in the women made by Walker-Hall was rejected by the women. An official Union paper *The Gazette* was started and official Union colours, blue and old gold, were adopted. McBain successfully negotiated with a Mr Chivers of Royal Promenade (now Queen's Road) for rooms above his shop. There was to be a reading room (32ft x 18½ft) and, in an adjoining room, a full-sized billiard table with a boy 'marker' in attendance. Meals were offered at 1*s*. (5p) for a 'hot plain lunch' with alternatives such as cold meat with bread for 8*d*. (3p) and bread and cheese for 3*d*. (1p) or with butter 4*d*. (1½p). The chair at all the early meetings, and most of the decisions, were taken by academic staff. A student of the time, J. E. Woodward, who became second secretary of the Union simply because his friend Warlow, the first secretary, left, did not recall massive student excitement. The new Union persisted in attempts to have both men and women in membership, but the women (under the tutelage of Miss Staveley) continued to object. There was an acrimonious correspondence since the women wanted to be called 'The Women's Union' and the men to be known as 'The Men's Union'. The men (under the tutelage of McBain) wanted a united union. In the end no-one won. When the University was formed it had, in its Charter, provision for a Guild of Undergraduates, but the Guild had a man President and a woman President and the men and women went on having rather separate existences: the women among their feminist portraits in their room at the top of the north wing, the men with Mr Chivers above his shop until after the First World War. The men then enjoyed a brief spell at the Royal Fort – their enjoyment indeed was excessive. According to Tyndall, they ran up an excess of expenditure over income of £1,700. The two halves of the Union were at last united in the Victoria Rooms in 1924; the separate Presidents lasted until 1971 when Jill Freeman became the first President to win an election open to men and women.

Murch and cricket team: *old Murch is the one with the broken arm.*

The founding of the Union was not the only blessing to flow from McBain and his colleagues of the Men's Lectures Committee. They also invented the Union Diary (in a form which remained virtually unchanged for 50 years) and a new magazine called *Nonesuch* (which went through various transformations from a staff edited magazine to a student edited weekly newspaper before winding up as the name of the student gossip column in the *Newsletter* over 60 years later). The Men's Lectures Committee also founded an Officers' Training Corps. Previously students like Woodward who were interested in military matters, or who thought it their duty, had joined the volunteers associated with the Gloucester Regiment. But perhaps the most important accomplishment of McBain and his colleagues, apart from the founding of the Union, was the creation of good sports facilities for the students.

The University College had made some steps in this direction, first at St Anne's and later at Horfield, but the grounds they leased and the accommodation – a wooden hut shared between the men's clubs and the ladies' hockey team – were very unsatisfactory. Prompted by McBain, Sir George Wills bought land from Frank Wedmore at Stoke Bishop (Coombe Dingle) and built a splendid pavilion there. Mr Wedmore warned Arrowsmith that the upkeep of the new sports field would be expensive. "You will not get a good labourer under 5*d*. (2p) or 6*d*. (2½p) per hour", he wrote, "and even then the best is the cheapest". The University had other distinguished advice about its sports staff. The great W. G. Grace wrote on 17 January 1911, "Murch is the very man for the job, if you can get him, as he knows how to make a cricket ground as well as anyone, and is a good coach as well". With such a recommendation the University could not do otherwise than appoint Billy Murch, an old Gloucestershire County bowler. Age and infirmity gradually made him less efficient and in 1927 he was

Bessant and Vint: *the team has a splendid line in blazers. Jack Bessant is standing far left in middle row and Jimmy Vint is seated second from right in front row.*

succeeded by Jack Bessant, another Gloucestershire County player who taught generations of Bristol cricketers to play with a straight bat. Strangely, they were taught to bowl by Jimmy Vint, a Mathematics lecturer who, even more bizarrely, was from Ireland, a country not renowned for cricket and where the national team was still playing in the 1970s as 'The Gentlemen of Ireland'. Bessant, who knew about such things, reckoned that Vint could have been a successful county player if he had devoted less time to scholarship and more to sport.

The advent of the new pavilion at Coombe Dingle was the cause of a Bristol riot. Soon after it was built, militant suffragettes, exhibiting that genius for selecting irrelevant and unsuitable targets which is characteristic of revolutionaries in the twentieth century, burned the place down. Incensed, so to speak, by this action, the men students attacked the suffragettes' headquarters, which was conveniently located across the road from the University.

Mrs M. Andrews, a student at the time, remembers, "The male students arranged to rush down University Road after 5.00 pm on the Friday and they reached the suffragette's shop in Queen's Road, threw out papers and pamphlets, threw in stink bombs and then lighted a huge bonfire in the middle of the road opposite the Museum and danced around it. There were crowds watching, but as the traffic was being held up the police sent for fire

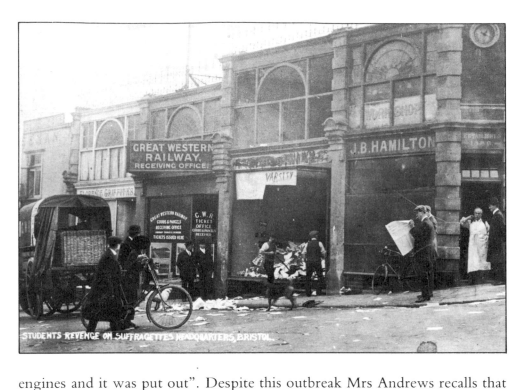

Retribution: *the Suffragettes' HQ in Queen's Road.*

Bedminster Hippodrome: *built by Oswald Stoll, it was the scene not only of student follies but of grand opera conducted by Thomas Beecham. Destroyed by enemy action, it was replaced by a cinema and is now converted to a warehouse and shop.*

engines and it was put out". Despite this outbreak Mrs Andrews recalls that students of that time were well-behaved. "It did not do to be seen walking down University Road by the Head Matron of Clifton Hill, let alone kissing and cuddling as I have seen recently (1975), but we were happy."

She also recalls that the first degree ceremonies were "more fun". The Engineers proceeded to the first degree ceremony mounted on donkeys and as each medical graduand was presented a student held a skeleton between the Vice-Chancellor (Sir Isambard Owen) and the graduand. On one occasion the police had cause to chase medical students into the newly built Coliseum in Park Row (where the Veterinary Anatomy building now stands). After one ceremony men students emerged to march to the Bedminster Hippodrome and take over the stage. The women marched but only watched the men's 'performance'. Mrs Andrews herself got into a row for putting up a notice on the Clifton Hill noticeboard about the event.

It was a happy time but it did not last. In 1914 war broke out and the new OTC started to send its men to the front. In 1913 it had a strength of two platoons (55 men). During the war 1,097 OTC men served, of whom 719 obtained commissions. 105 students lost their lives and 121 honours were obtained including one Victoria Cross.

Hardy Falconer Parsons was the son of the Rev. J. A. Ash Parsons, the Pastor of Old King Street Chapel in Bristol. Like Chesterman, his exact

Lieutenant Hardy Parsons VC.

contemporary, he wanted to be a medical missionary. Chesterman was to survive both world wars and become a very distinguished medical missionary rating a major obituary in *The Times* when he died in 1983. Hardy Parsons joined the OTC and was later posted to the cadet battalion at Oxford. Although deemed unfit for service he volunteered for service with the 'Bantam' battalion of the Gloucestershire Regiment. He was not misled by any dreams of glory. He hated war but believed it was his duty to serve. In August 1917 he died gallantly in action. His citation for the Victoria Cross reads:

> "*Second-Lieutenant H. F. Parsons (14th Battalion).* For most conspicuous bravery during a night attack by a strong party of the enemy on a bombing post held by his command on 21 August 1917. The bombers holding the block were forced back, but Second-Lieutenant Parsons remained at his post, and, single-handed and although severely scorched and burnt by liquid fire, he continued to hold up the enemy with bombs until severely wounded.
>
> "This very gallant act of self-sacrifice and devotion to duty undoubtedly delayed the enemy long enough to allow of the organisation of a bombing party, which succeeded in driving back the enemy before they could enter any portion of the trenches.
>
> "This gallant officer succumbed to his wounds."

When the war was over, his fellow students marched in procession to the Downs to witness his parents' receiving his medal from the hands of the King himself.

During the war the absence of the young men fighting and dying at the front had an effect on the University. In Chemistry, for example, Garner noted that the number of students in the Department was halved, the honours school disappeared and research decreased to practically zero. There were other interruptions. Edward Livingstone joined the University Zoology Department in 1915. He remembered, "In 1916 the Military took over the Arts Department (then in the section facing Woodland Road) and the staff and students were transferred to the Baptist College. In the Quadrangle (now a car park) was built a very large hut (the cook house) and the large hall became the dining room. About a year later the OTC were moved and the Royal Flying Corps took over. The cook house became a workshop and in the large hall aeroplanes were demonstrated".*

Life for the remaining students was not easy. Gladys Hart was a student in Clifton Hill. She remembered, "Meals were a problem at that time of food rationing. There were, I remember, small scales on the dining room tables so that students could verify that they were not eating more than their fair share of bread. A favourite pudding – alas, it was served all too rarely – was a turnover pie made from potato flour and containing a filling of mashed potato soaked in treacle. We loved spam – but how rarely we saw it . . . we tried not to be greedy and went hopefully to cocoa parties for scraps of nourishment".

Part of the way through Miss Hart's first year the war ended and the students danced in the streets. She remembered, "Until demobilisation really got going women students far outnumbered the men, except in the Engineering Department. The Medical School attracted many women. The war had created a revolution in surgery and there was an ever-growing demand for the services of the new women doctors".

Among the ranks of these new women medical students was Victoria Tryon. Many years later the University conferred on her the honorary degree of MA but in 1919 she was President of the Union. Union minutes reveal that it was she who proposed and organised the revival of student misbehaviour during degree congregations. This bizarre behaviour continued through the 1920s. Walter Norman Booker recorded his impressions of the 1927 degree in his diary:

"*Sat July 2nd.* Attended the Degree Congregation which was timed for 11.30 am. We had to be ready at 11.00 am and while waiting had a fine scrum in the space between the main stairs; the visitors were looking over the balustrading above and laughing at us. When the Congregation opened Lord Haldane rose and before he could say anything the awed silence was broken by an undergrad's great shout, 'What a jolly fine hat!', referring to his mortar-board with gold braid and gold tassel. From this time on there was a continuous fire of comments; one medical going up to the platform and coming down again was greeted with roar after roar of 'Take those spats off'. The clock striking 12 was quite drowned by the imitated hum of its reverberation. Another graduate returning to his place was greeted by, 'The more we are together the merrier we shall be'. A hen was let loose and fled 30 – 40 ft over our heads; a child's balloon went up, besides papers in the air. When some ladies went up to receive degrees of PhD their bright red robes with purple sleeves and hoods with white centres caused cries of, 'The latest creation!'. One lady being handed to the Chancellor to receive an Honorary Degree and afterwards being handed down the stairs ceremoniously by a member of the staff acting as an usher, there were loud cries of, 'Oh! Oh! TK-TK-TK. Oh! Oh!', besides the humming of a dance tune. When the procession went out at the end the professors passed thro' a running fire of comments. The Vice-Chancellor sent down a message about half-way thro' the honorary degrees for silence. Yet on the whole it went off very quietly. There were very many visitors present; the whole hall was filled."

(The Union Council was informed that on future occasions "While rowdyism was discouraged the University authorities were not averse to witty remarks".)

This rowdyism was more characteristic of 'Rag' activities. The ostensible reason for the 'Rag' was to raise money for Bristol hospitals, but for the men

The General Strike 1926. *Bristol students, when they were involved at all, backed the employers.*

Rag. *Rag has not changed much over the years. Costumes of the 1930s were repeated in the 1950s.*

Winston Churchill *was a popular choice as Chancellor and his arrival was greeted in a 'rag' fashion. The Chancellor, fortified by a mid-morning brandy at the Vice-Chancellor's house, was conveyed down Blackboy Hill to the Victoria Rooms. He was borne shoulder high into the Union.*

Blazers: *colours were important . . .*

Blazers: *. . . for both sexes.*

students it was an opportunity to dress in funny clothes and behave outrageously. Women students, often clothed in cap and gown, seem to have confined their role to that of spectator. By 1925 the Union had established a 'Rag Damages' fund which was frequently called upon despite the best efforts of the Vice-Chancellor and the police to enforce order. L. R. Philips, President in 1927, was warned by the Vice-Chancellor and the Chief Constable that if there were any misdemeanours on the part of the Union's members, *he* would be immediately arrested. The deterrent did not work and a ceremonial bonfire was lighted outside the Victoria Rooms seriously damaging the pavement.

But time produced the desired result. In 1929 'Rag' was banned as 'not being in accordance with the dignity of the University'. Union minutes record great debates about faculty and university colours; perhaps as a symbol of the new sobriety, in 1929 the Union agreed to change the colour of the University blazer from Bristol red to black. In 1931 the Union established that the colours for the University's faculties should be: Medicine (red), Arts and Education (blue), Engineering (green), and Science (yellow). They called upon the University to reflect this in the colours chosen for faculty prospectuses. On 20 March 1931, they appointed T. C. Marsh as University outfitters.

In common with students in many other universities, the Bristol Union began to take an interest in international affairs. The Bristol Union had established compulsory membership of all students in the University on 22 February 1921. In May 1922 Bristol joined the infant National Union of Students. The chief benefit the National Union offered was cheap travel; the chief duty it demanded was an interest in international affairs, a reflection of the personal interests of Iveson McAdam, an ex-soldier who was its founder and first President. The first NUS conference held in the provinces was held at Bristol in 1927. At that time Bristol students were not politically very aware and it was not until the early 1930s that politically concerned students forced a successful vote in the General Meeting which persuaded the membership, against the advice of the Presidents, to send a delegate to an 'International Student Congress against War and Fascism in Brussels'. Interest in war and peace grew as the 1930s progressed. One correspondent in *Nonesuch* noted sadly that while 'the imperialist press' complained that Britain was spending £540 a day on the League of Nations, the Government was spending about £200 a minute preparing for war. The future war, the same correspondent averred, would happen "so quickly that unless some independent person agreed to give the 'GO!', it would be almost impossible to put up any defence". A Peace Council and an Anti-War Society were formed in the Union, and the views of students were earnestly sought in a questionnaire which asked, *inter alia,* "Do you agree that unilateral disarmament for Great Britain is (a) Desirable, (b) Practicable, (c) Wholly,

(d) Partially?". The results were: 116 desirable; 98 undesirable; 117 unpracticable; 59 partially practicable; 35 wholly practicable. Individual comments on the questionnaire called for Britain to take the lead as an act of faith. Others believed such a course would be suicidal. One respondent did not record his view but he thought it was "a fantastic question". It's a pity one doesn't know whether his use of English was deliberate or merely ironic slang.

But it would be a mistake to regard the 1930s in Bristol as a time of a great student peace movement. There was such a movement certainly and its language and its concerns may seem to be repeated today but the 1930s also saw the emergence of two other great student traditions – apathy and frivolous enjoyment. The apathy is widely mentioned by successive editors of *Nonesuch*. One writer even predicted the end of the Union and its societies. He complained, "The only way a Union society can succeed is to scrap its "aims" and give a bun fight, and an entertainment by the committee afterwards".

Entertainment was attractive to students. Most major societies gave balls and there was a good deal of inter-university entertaining at the Union Ball. The Presidents of the Bristol Union would be invited to Union Balls in other universities. When its turn came, Bristol invited the other Presidents. Elaborate menu cards were produced for the accompanying dinners and at most dances, cards were used. Each dance (foxtrot, waltz and so on) was listed and the first 15 minutes of every function was occupied in filling up one's card. Even if one went to the dance with a partner it was expected that all but four dances (especially not the dance immediately before supper) would be assigned to someone else. These student-organised dances were attended by the staff and the Vice-Chancellor frequently danced the supper dance with the lady President. These formal dances remained a feature of university life until the late 1950s when they began to die out but in Bristol at least the Medical students continued to have a ball into the 1970s – in 1968, the year of the great sit-in, the Medical Ball was organised at a country club near Bristol as a deliberate affront to the 'political students' who had denied the revellers the use of the Union building.

The advent of the Second World War provided a temporary break in the formality of these occasions. There was no longer the paper, the dress material or the food to support them. Curiously, the numbers of students were not a problem. In fact, as *Nonesuch* observed, the chief effect of the war on student Bristol was to double everything: "It had doubled the student body of the University, doubled our Union, and made our rooms in hall double rooms". The reason for the doubling was that King's College, London was evacuated to Bristol. For the duration of the conflict two universities occupied the City. For the Engineers, at Unity Street which was also the home of the Merchant Venturers' Technical College, there were

A Dance Card.

Dances and Balls. *The invitations from one university union to another were often elaborately and colourfully printed. Full evening dress (with tails for men) was worn to dances and dinners.*

treble problems, exacerbated at times by the presence among the King's contingent of a deranged technician who occasionally ran about chasing people with a knife. Life was hard but it had its compensations. The Union had to put up 'black-out' curtains which it was claimed rendered parts of it accessible only to experienced members of the Spelaeological Club, but women students started wearing trousers publicly for the first time. Even if tea at Clifton Hill were occasionally jamless and the *Daily Sketch* and *Sunday Pictorial* were no longer found in the common room, there were *men* in residence on the roof as fire-watchers. Men were allowed to visit the Hall for tea after 1939, and the heroic souls on the roof at night, of course, had to be plied with warming drinks. At Clifton Hill and Manor Hall many girl students suddenly discovered the novel view of the University which was to be had from the fire-watcher's aery vantage point.

The student fire-watchers (who included in their number a future Vice-Chancellor, Alec Merrison) did an effective job. When the Coliseum was bombed a group of students led by the Assistant Librarian, Shum Cox, saved the University's Library. King's College was less fortunate: its library, removed from London for safe-keeping, was destroyed when the Great Hall was bombed. Students at Unity Street saved their building and then saved other buildings opposite by turning their pressure hoses on them. Next morning, some of the owners were less than grateful. The students, they complained had used "too much water".

In 1946, when the King's College students, accompanied by their mascot Reggie the lion, returned to London, Bristol welcomed 55 men from the United States Army. Several Americans subsequently took Bristol girls with them as their wives. One of them, Jerome E. Klein, wrote, "This spring, as the leaves begin to turn green in our own parks, we shall remember the Downs, College Green, and the lovely park about Cabot Tower, and we shall have nostalgic memories of you, with whom we shared our most pleasant hours overseas, while we were G.I. students at Bristol University".

For the Bristol students themselves, the pattern of pre-war life began to re-assert itself. In the 1930s Bernard Lovell's recreation had been cricket, music-making, long conversations with staff and fellow students over tea in Bright's. Tony Flint, a research student in the immediate post-war years, lists exactly the same activities plus some agreeable rural weekends at the country cottage of his professor, Alfred Pugsley.

'Rag', and its occasional excesses, was restored but there were a number of significant changes. After the formation of the NHS, the proceeds of the collection and other fund-raising events were no longer for hospital funds; they were applied to more general charitable purposes which varied from year to year. More extensive use was made of the 'Immunity Badge' system. This was a sort of 'protection racket': any shop, office or individual wearing a badge was not to be assaulted. There was a further difference: the women

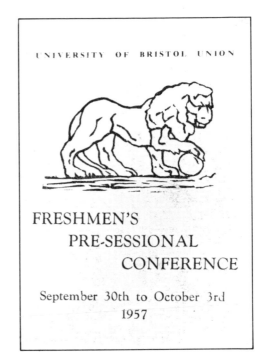

UNIVERSITY OF BRISTOL UNION

FRESHMEN'S
PRE-SESSIONAL
CONFERENCE

September 30th to October 3rd
1957

Reggie the Lion *the mascot of King's College, London. A replica, Reggie Minimus, was given to Bristol in gratitude for war-time hospitality.*

The Skiffle Groups. *The chief merit was that the instruments were cheap; the bass here was acquired from the Refectory.*

Bristol at War. *A Rag 'battle' in the city centre.*

students now participated fully in the general rowdyism, dressing-up and horse-play. 'Rag' acquired national dimensions through inter-university raids and other stunts to attract press publicity. Lady Presidents across the country and Union mascots were particular targets of 'kidnap' attempts. In the manner of Roman triumphs, such captives were featured in 'Rag' processions. There were also pre-arranged set-piece battles. In 1955 a 'war' between Bristol, Birmingham and Southampton consumed 60 cases of rotten fruit from the Bristol market plus quantities of soot, water and fireworks. The inter-varsity balls and dinners resumed. So too, curiously, did the dance cards for formal occasions. Ordinary student dances were completely informal. Dancing to skiffle groups or traditional jazz bands was not of the kind which permitted dance cards. Jive or 'skip jive' (known to elders of the time by the pre-war term 'jitter-bugging') to be practised at the highest level demanded experienced partners used to the choreography improvised by the man. *Nonesuch* reported in 1955, "To say that dancing is popular in the University is a statement lacking in evidence. Rather it can be said that the so-called dances are popular, or standing like sardines that were not quite killed when they were pickled or *vice versa*". It was decided to form a ballroom dancing club to preserve the old skills of the foxtrot and the waltz.

Inter-university debates received a boost when *The Observer* newspaper started a competition for '*The Observer* Mace'. Inter-university drama received a similar quasi-official stimulus when *The Sunday Times* started a drama festival. The Edinburgh Festival fringe, which grew throughout the 1950s, gradually drew more and more student groups into fierce 'free market' competition. In all three Bristol groups enjoyed great success.

There was even a revival of practical jokes and hoaxes. In November 1955 four freshers arrived at Temple Meads, having boarded the London train at Bath, as a 'student delegation from the University of Kiev' to be greeted by a Reception Committee, representatives of two Bristol newspapers, and officials of the Union 'Democratic Society'. Short speeches on East-West tension were exchanged – the 'Russian delegation' declining the services of an interpreter. The following day the delegation toured Avonmouth and nearly destroyed their whole carefully wrought illusion by giggling on the way to a bus stop when their limousine failed to materialise. The hoax (by Brian Walton, Brian Richards, David Davies and Maria Edmond) worked because British towns and cities had become used to greeting such delegations. A year later, with Russia's invasion of Hungary, it would have been impossible. The Hungarian revolt coincided with the Suez war: like students everywhere, the Bristol students debated the issue. The Victoria Rooms was packed and when the vote was taken there was a narrow majority against the Conservative Government of the day. But the Suez vote was not a reflection of the political attitudes of the Union. The Conservatives

The Great Russian Hoax.

won a 'mock election' very easily: the left-wing element among students was small. These political attitudes were not surprising at the time. There was a strong public school element among the students, and Bristol had begun to achieve its 'first after Oxbridge' status in the applications for admission made by sixth-formers. *Nonesuch News* (now a weekly paper) reported over one-third of Bristol students had a grant of £50 or less. Many of them had no grant at all. A student's chances of obtaining a grant depended entirely on where he lived in the country. Some local education authorities would not provide more than a limited number of grants in any one year. Nevertheless the numbers of students from the Bristol area continued to fall. By the middle 1950s the percentage of 'Bristol area' students had fallen to 25%: in the next decade it was to fall further. In terms of its student population Bristol was becoming a national University. This change in the place of origin of the students produced changes in the University organisation because the University now stood *in loco parentis* to large numbers of students living away from home. In health care, for example, the Students' Health Service (one of the first in a British university) now accepted all students as patients and gave each one a health check on entry. Accommodation became more organised. In the very early days the University College's efforts had been confined to a list held by the Registrar. The creation of Clifton Hill and Canynge Halls demonstrated the benefits of halls of residence. In the late

Bristol Fashion. *Bristol students have always admired style. A 1950s Engineering student found it in dress but perhaps the most peculiar instance of it was achieved by a young aristocratic student of the 1930s. According to the writer Patricia Daly, a student of the time, he had his man-servant sit School Certificate and accompany him as a fellow-student to Bristol.*

1920s Manor Hall and Wills Hall improved the accommodation available, and after the war Burwalls and Langford were added to the men's halls.

Dr Millicent Taylor became Accommodation Officer in the late 1940s with a duty to see and approve lodgings. All University accommodation was rationalised and the quasi-independent status enjoyed by Clifton Hill was ended. By the session 1954-55 the dimensions of the accommodation problem were clearly demonstrable. In that year there were 355 men in hall, 44 in theological colleges, 1,015 in lodgings and 364 at home; there were 296 women in hall, 476 in lodgings and 117 at home. The projected numbers for the remainder of the 1950s and the 1960s meant that, at Bristol as elsewhere, there would need to be a massive building programme. The lodgings and the existing halls, indeed the existing Students' Union, manifestly could not cope.

But all these were problems for the Vice-Chancellor and the University's officers; for the students in the late 1950s the problems were more immediate. Elizabeth Marleyn (née Woods) recalls:

"On the whole we took work pretty seriously, and there were few drop-outs. We were not very career conscious since there were plenty of jobs going at that time, and teaching was the soft option. I think I was one of three in my English school year who did *not* go on to do the Education year. There was certainly no question of student participation in running university affairs financially or academically – though we all detested Anglo-Saxon, no-one ever dared make representations to the Professor about dropping it from the course.

"Nor were we all that money conscious. My grant was £175 a year to start with and went up to £250 when I was a postgraduate. My rent for the flat was 30s. a week and food cost the same. We spent less on clothes; I think because young fashion didn't exist and there was less pressure to look trendy. But proportionately we spent a lot more on books, because so few were in paperback. In my last year as a postgraduate I spent £80 out of my £250 on books. We walked or biked everywhere and spent virtually nothing on bus fares. Very few students had cars. Contact with teaching staff socially was minimal: I can only remember once visiting the home of my supervisor for the two years when I was doing research, and I never met the Professor socially.

"There seemed to be more student union clubs then, with the emphasis on sport, caving, rambling, mountaineering etc and hobbies – stamps, chess, geology, music. The choral society was about 500 strong. The Christians were rife, BIFCU, and evangelical too, always pestering you to come on Christian rambles and quiet time meetings, and this element was particularly strong in the halls of residence, where there were optional prayers every day. There were no minority political groups, just the odd Communist, and no

philosophies to be 'into' at the time, no Zen, no I Ching, no vegetarianism, and if we studied Marxism, it was in an academic context.

"On the whole we were a pretty unsophisticated lot, the reason being I think that the teenage cult had not started, and that we had all been very insulated from the world at school, and just found University a freer version of school: we were conservative and unquestioning through conditioning at school, and being the war baby generation, were used to austerity and so maybe less materialistic than the students of the 1960s, and more passive."

The 1960s brought the new halls – Churchill, Hiatt Baker, Badock, and Goldney with extensions at Wills, Clifton Hill, and Langford. Over 40% of Bristol students were able to live in accommodation provided by the University. The restrictive rules about visitors and late passes were relaxed. When the age of majority was reduced to 18 the University no longer stood *in loco parentis*. The 1960s also brought to Bristol a splendid new six-storey Union building with a much-needed University swimming pool in the basement. There was a purpose-built theatre/debating chamber, ample committee rooms, dark rooms for photography, quiet rooms for prayer and the longest bar in the country. (This particular piece of *hubris* was appropriately punished: the beer didn't improve in the long pipes the length of the bar demanded. Given a choice of stale beer or a more efficient size, the students shortened the bar.) Students' grants improved (the NUS still

Engineers' Inventiveness. *The fuel crisis produced by the 1956 Suez crisis caused the Government to issue petrol coupons. The Engineers ensured that their Ball tickets had an essential look to them.*

The OTC. *In the 1950s women students were allowed to join the Officers' Training Corps but after a few years were banned again by the War Minister. The Minister in question was John Profumo, who had to resign because of the 'Christine Keeler affair'. His decision was later rescinded.*

Hungry students in the days of the University College had to seek their food in the cafés and restaurants in Queen's Road and Park Street. Some were rather unsalubrious but the splendid Bonnets was a special treat in the first two decades of the century. The Museum café and The Berkeley were the favourite haunts of staff and students between the wars. After the Second World War Ralph Brentnall adapted the old City Museum to provide a refectory which was very popular, particularly at lunchtimes. The Berkeley, however, continued to attract the coffee table intellectuals and its closure was a great blow to University conversation.

regards 1963-64 as the high-water mark in student support). Never had the material comforts and welfare of students been so high.

Into this paradise there came a generation of students who rejected it all. They questioned the relevance of the new academic disciplines the University offered; they demanded a say in the way they were taught. They rejected the high academic standards and the concern for truth which Bristol had established. They rejected too the traditional fun. In 1971 the Union President Jill Freeman said, "There is a general feeling that Rag has had its day . . . We are discussing the idea of a community festival". The Union Ball and the Union Dinner were ended; instead of the formal yet convivial contacts between Presidents at dinners, there were now urgent conspiracies between Unions against 'reactionary' Vice-Chancellors and frenzied plotting of common tactics in the pursuit of 'issues' and 'campaigns'. The traditional regard between students and those who worked for them broke down. (In the 1950s relations were so friendly there was actually a bye-law forbidding students to buy porters drinks). The first sit-in occurred as a result of students' disregard of Union porters' wish to go home at the end of a long day's work; the last sit-in of the troubled period (in support of a nursery action campaign) saw students actually attack University porters at Senate House. Relations with academic staff were hardly better, although they were sometimes marked by a curious ambivalence. At one student demonstration a protestor shouted a particularly offensive piece of abuse at his Professor (Stefan Körner, at that time a Pro-Vice-Chancellor and involved in that capacity). The next day the student came up to Professor Körner in his department. "I want to assure you, Sir,", he said, "there was nothing personal intended in the remark I made to you yesterday."

The students who thought and behaved thus were a minority. A student President of the time, Paul Vollans, who resigned rather than lead them, believed that they numbered no more than 70. This was a smaller number than the members of the Ballroom Dancing Club, and a third of the members of the Equestrian Club, both of which flourished in the same period. Yet this determined 1% of the student body for a period of six or seven years managed to persuade the press and public that they spoke for students in Bristol, and because the same thing was happening elsewhere, in the nation. The true spirit of the undergraduates remained submerged – students still acted in plays, competed in debates, drank coffee in the Berkeley Café, and studied hard and passed examinations but these activities, because unreported, did not exist in the public eye. Even when the Engineers, in an interesting revival of typical 1950s 'Rag' raiding, attacked a sit-in, captured its red flag and distributed it in tiny squares as souvenirs, press reporters remained unmoved.

Such aberrant behaviour in students could not and did not last. In 1978 normality was restored by the election as the chief officers of the Union, of a

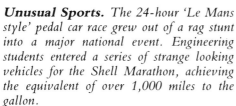

Unusual Sports. *The 24-hour 'Le Mans style' pedal car race grew out of a rag stunt into a major national event. Engineering students entered a series of strange looking vehicles for the Shell Marathon, achieving the equivalent of over 1,000 miles to the gallon.*

group of students who believed in fun. Led by a white West Indian, Chris Hamel-Smith, they called themselves the Epicureans. Their attempt to establish frivolity as a ruling principle failed in the long run: the tradition of student apathy was too well-established. The only permanent and visible evidence of the dreary years of dispute and the short period of reaction now is the names of two bars in the Union: the Mandela Bar, named by unworthy people in honour of a worthy man, and the Epicurean Bar. The invisible effects, like the destruction of public confidence in universities and many ordinary students' willingness to participate actively in the life of the Union, may take a long time to restore. Traditions, once broken, are difficult to re-establish.

The Union and the corporate life of students of course is only one part of the history of students in Bristol. There is also the history of individual students, of that legion of people who could say "I was a Bristol student". In the 100 or more years since the University College was founded, or the 75 since the University received its Charter, there have been many who have graduated and gone on to successful careers in industry and commerce, as leaders and doctors, lawyers and scientists, architects and social scientists. But there are some who for one reason or another have come into the public eye. They are, fame aside, typical of the many.

In the early days of the University College, two of Rowley's pupils, Katharine Bradley and her niece Edith Cooper, who wrote together as Michael Field and Miss Higginson who wrote as Moira O'Neill, established national reputations in literature. McLain, one of Hele Shaw's pupils, went to the USA where, although he had no degree, the breadth of his training led him to a career in power stations before being called out of retirement to work on rockets in the Second World War. Watt, a holder of one the Daimler scholarships in automobile engineering despised by Flexner, was called back by the University from Coventry where he was working on the Royal car, to be offered a post in the old house at Filton where the new Bristol and Colonial Airplane Company (BAC) was being established. His first job, under Coanda, the French technical director, was to design a propeller. The characteristic breadth of Bristol engineering, and its fascination with the design and testing of engineering structures, led him into aircraft design. With Lieutenant Hope he designed the first British flying boat. Later Watt concentrated his attention on propellers and left the wings and other structures to Sutton Pippard, a fellow student at University College. From airplane structures in the First World War, Pippard went on, by way of a peacetime career of numerous distinctions as a civil engineer, to design self-sealing petrol tanks, and floating airfields, and to make substantial contributions to the Bailey Bridge invented during the Second World War.

For some students, particularly the women, their achievement was that they were not just pioneers: they were the first. Dr Adams, for example, was one of the first women to qualify in the Bristol Medical School (1911): she was not allowed, by social convention, to sleep overnight at the hospital or to use the men's dining room. She persevered in her medical tasks and dismissed the rest of it with the comment, "I became terribly thin because I could not get enough to eat". The redoubtable Victoria Tryon, as first woman resident of the General Hospital, broke down all the barriers to women in the 1920s. Mrs Andrews, following the Ramsay tradition of 'learning by doing something new' (a tradition Ramsay learnt from Lord Kelvin, who spoke at the Victoria Rooms meeting of 1874) and under the direction of Priestley, read a paper in Botany at a British Association meeting, an event unusual for the time in three particulars: she was a woman, a woman scientist, and still a student.

There have been students whose careers in the University have not been renowned for scholarship. Arnold Ridley was a somewhat reluctant student before the First World War who had come to the University with the vague idea of becoming a teacher. When the war broke out he abandoned his degree and joined up. When the conflict ended, he was about to resume his studies when he was offered a job in the theatre with the famous Miss Horniman. For Ridley the choice was simple. He became a very successful playwright – one play in particular, *The Ghost Train,* is a classic and is still widely

Television Stars. *Arnold Ridley portrayed one of the most-loved characters on television as Private Godfrey in* Dad's Army; *Tim Pigott-Smith enjoyed higher rank in* Jewel in the Crown *but was everyone's favourite villain.*

Nicolette Milnes Walker in mid-Atlantic.

The first black President. George Odlum, with the Lady President of the Union, greets the Queen and the Duke of Edinburgh. He is now a leading politician in his own country.

produced. In his old age he became a major television star as 'Private Godfrey' in the BBC series *Dad's Army*.

Other later students have also won fame in television. Sue Lawley, President of the Union in 1967, reads the news for the BBC, and Alastair Stewart, Vice-President in 1973, reads the news for ITN. Elizabeth Horrocks was the first woman to win BBC's *Mastermind* competition, and the Royal Shakespeare Company's Tim Pigott-Smith is now a leading television actor.

The printed word media have also seen some notable 'firsts'. Julie Welch, who won a student journalism prize for reporting the beginnings of the 'student revolution', became the nation's first top rank woman sports reporter and the first woman to write with authority in a national newspaper about football. Nicolette Milnes Walker made the news when she became the first woman to sail single-handed across the North Atlantic.

Other Bristol students have made news. President Yusuf Lule of Uganda, the first Bristol graduate to become head of state, unfortunately was quickly deposed by a revolution. George Odlum, the first black President of the Union, has had a more fortunate career. In November 1979 he was made Deputy Prime Minister of Saint Lucia, and also Minister for Trade, Industry, Tourism, Information, Broadcasting, Statistics and Foreign Affairs. Currently he is leader of the party in opposition, the Progressive Labour

A repaired Lion. Colin Patterson, the Irish Rugby International, Bristol's first representative in the British Lions team, was injured in South Africa. His damaged knee was repaired using a tendon replacement technique pioneered at Langford for horses.

The Ha–Ha Game. Out at Langford the Ha-Ha game played by Veterinary students had only one rule: thou shalt not kill.

Happy Endings. *As student life ends at a graduation garden party, addresses are swopped and promises to keep in touch are made.*

Party (since 1982). Another black student, Paul Boateng, a Bristol lawyer, is now a major leader of the black communities in London. Hugh Bayley, a Union President in the troubled 1970s, leads a London Borough. Andy Pott, Treasurer in 1971, leads Avon County Council. A former sit-in leader, Rebecca Johnson, is prominent among the Greenham Common women.

Curiously, Bristol has produced few major Parliamentary politicians in Britain. Michael Cocks, a frequent but unsuccessful contender for Union President in the 1950s, as Chief Whip of the Labour Party, is the only recent one to have attained Cabinet rank, although many Bristol graduates have managed to gain election to the House of Commons. Whatever students learn at Bristol, it seems to persuade most of them to make their contributions in other, quieter ways. Among these we may number Sue Lloyd, the current editor of Roget's *Thesaurus*.

But whatever their calling, or their fame, the students the University has produced more than justify the faith and hope of those whose vision created the idea of a university for Bristol over a hundred years ago.

Chapter Nine

University Buildings

When the Wills brothers told George Oatley that the memorial building to their father should last 400 years, they were making academic and architectural as well as filial statements. The Wills Memorial Building was to be not just a Wills family 'pyramid', to set alongside the Museum and Art Gallery as a sign of their generosity to the citizens of Bristol: it was to be an institutional symbol of permanence for "the University for Bristol" (the preposition is important) which their father had mentioned in his letter offering his crucial donation to the Charter campaign. Their aim, on the whole, was successful. For most Bristolians, the Wills Memorial Building *is* the University.

A symbol of academic permanence was needed: throughout its history the University College had never enjoyed financial stability. Its building developments, while occasionally ambitious in intention, had always had to be phased and, as with most phased schemes, in the end the totality of the scheme was never achieved. The first buildings in Park Row (ironically until their occupation by the College an Asylum for the Deaf) were hopeless as long-term prospects and the College Council commissioned Jethro Cossins, who designed Mason's College, Birmingham (afterwards Birmingham University), to design their new University College. Cossins' ideas proved to be unacceptable and several local architects were asked to submit designs. A design by Charles Hansom, younger brother of Joseph Hansom, the inventor of the Hansom cab, was chosen.

On the right scale, Hansom's building would have given Bristol an imposing building, suitably academic in appearance, and perhaps a little like Keble College in total impact although dissimilar in details. In practice, however, the scale was much too small and the College Council could not afford even that – only the north wing of Hansom's proposed quadrangle was in the first phase completed in 1880. The eastern side, the back of the quadrangle, was completed in 1883. The south wing, begun in 1893, was not completed until 1904. The imposing gate-tower on the University Road frontage was abandoned and when Oatley added a little tower in memory of Albert Fry to the north wing, it was announced in the local press that the

Old Museum. *The old city Museum, one of Bristol's finest Victorian gothic buildings, is now the University Refectory.*

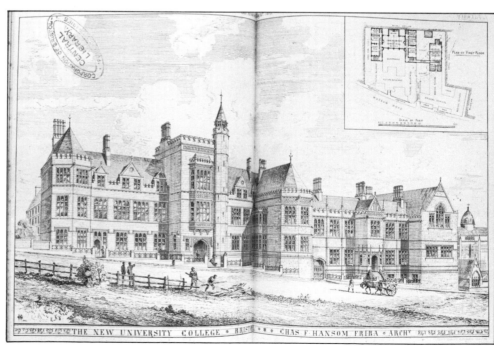

Hansom Design. *The published drawing showing what the University College would have looked like had funds been available.*

building was complete. By then the addition of the Medical block, designed by F. Bligh Bond in much the same style of Tudoresque Gothic, had destroyed the totality of Hansom's design.

The accommodation provided was quite good – Ramsay liked his laboratory in the centre of the back block particularly – but the College had not succeeded in imposing its presence upon the city. When Travers arrived, for example, he found that, for many Bristolians, "the College" meant Clifton College and it was to that institution rather than the University Road structures that enquirers were most frequently directed.

The first building erected after the granting of the Charter by the new University did little to alter the College's 'lack of image'. It was an extension of the Hansom buildings north to the Woodland Road side. Oatley, the architect, managed to provide (1910) useful laboratory space and a memorial tower to J. W. Arrowsmith in an idiom consonant with the existing buildings. This development used up all the sites available to the University with two exceptions, the delightful garden created by Leipner at the most northerly part of the University Road/Woodland Road triangle, and the Blind Asylum site on Queen's Road.

The Blind Asylum was the site identified for the Wills Memorial Building. It was made larger by the purchase of the Rifle Drill Hall, for many years the centre for Bristol entertainments such as Hengler's Circus. George Wills built another hall in Old Market to provide an alternative venue for such events. The steep slope to Woodland Road, the desirability of link doors to the new Museum and Art Gallery, and the 'gap' at the top of Park Street were all problems for the architect to solve.

Writing in 1976 Roger Gill said, "The design was remarkable. In size and exuberance it far surpasses any secular building in the City. It is matched only by the Cathedral and St Mary Redcliffe. The 215 feet high tower with the fourth largest bell in Britain, the vast entrance hall, the massive double staircase, the Great Hall, the Reception Room and the Council Chamber have few equals as a ceremonial setting. It is a monument to the Wills family, a salute to the Princes Academical, and profligate with space. The quality of the fabric is superb, the detail is accurate, but the ambience of a mediaeval university is strangely lacking. It is a sham, an imposing sham; so imposing that it must be placed high on the list of British follies for which many have high regard and affection. For others, a sham only arouses feelings of discomfort, and in this instance feelings of regret that so much money was spent on building, when so little money was available for books, equipment, laboratories and staff. Academic humility is one quality not recorded in these stones."

Had Gill been writing 30 years earlier his judgement might have been more harsh; it was fashionable to regret this building until Pevsner gave it his approval. But even Gill's qualified criticism is hardly fair. The building was

The University's first building. *The first building to be completed after the Charter, the present Zoology and Botany Departments, was opened with due ceremony.*

Park Street *before the Wills Memorial Building.*

Closing the Gap. *Oatley's 1911 drawing of his projected masterpiece.*

The University's Shield. *There is no justification for the fasces used as supporters.*

designed to solve the technical problems of the site: it has to be admitted there is little sense of the slope's influence inside the structure. The grand staircase seems to grow naturally as a ceremonial route from the door and foyer where one is unaware of the sheer weight of the external structure of the tower. The link to the museum determined the use of the western side of the building; most of the everyday teaching space is located to the east yet the building does not feel notably asymmetric.

The memorial aspects of the building (and it is after all a memorial) are confined to the splendid entrance. The Founders' Window (a new design, the original Founder's window having been destroyed by enemy action) records armorially the Wills family, the University, the City of Bristol, the Society of Merchant Venturers, the old counties of Wiltshire, Somerset and Gloucestershire, Balliol College, New College, Percival, Fry, Hobhouse, Haldane, Leverhulme, Worsley and Abbot. The armorials above the staircase represent the University (motto: *Vim promovet insitam* – learning promotes the innate powers); George Wills (motto: *Pro aris et focis* – literally 'for our altars and hearths', freely 'for God and our homes'); and Harry Wills (motto: *Quo lux ducit* – 'where light leads'). Even those to whom memorials are distasteful would no doubt agree that this record of the University's benefactors and founders is appropriate and, since the significance of the armorials is not immediately obvious to every lay man, discreet. The aims inherent in the mottos are also beyond reproach for a University, particularly if one adds to them those carved in the Reception Room: *Vinum et musica laetificant cor* and *et super utraque dilectio sapientiae* which rendered freely is 'Wine and music delight the heart but the love of wisdom is better than both of them'. The detail of the building is not only accurate, as Gill suggests; it is also genuinely witty. Oatley and Jean Hahn, the sculptor, discussed the detail of the grotesques (they were not properly speaking gargoyles) and there are portrait masks of Lloyd Morgan and other worthies, but there is also one figure who can only be "Old Father Kruschen", a popular figure in commercial advertising of the period. The appearance of *fasces* as supporters of the University arms in the Council Chamber may seem politically odd but Oatley's Tudor electric clocks are delightful and it is a great pity that the fire which destroyed the Great Hall also destroyed the wood carvings which decorated the tops of the linen-fold panels: the designs that have survived are charming.

The practical detail of the building is no less impressive. Harry Wills had been trained as an engineer and he took a keen, informed and detailed interest in buildings (the portrait in the Reception Room shows him holding a set of plans). According to Tyndall, he was a man whom it was difficult to drive and impossible to lead. He had views on construction no argument could shake. One such view was that all fittings and materials should be of such quality that no repairs should be required for over 50 years. Thus, in the

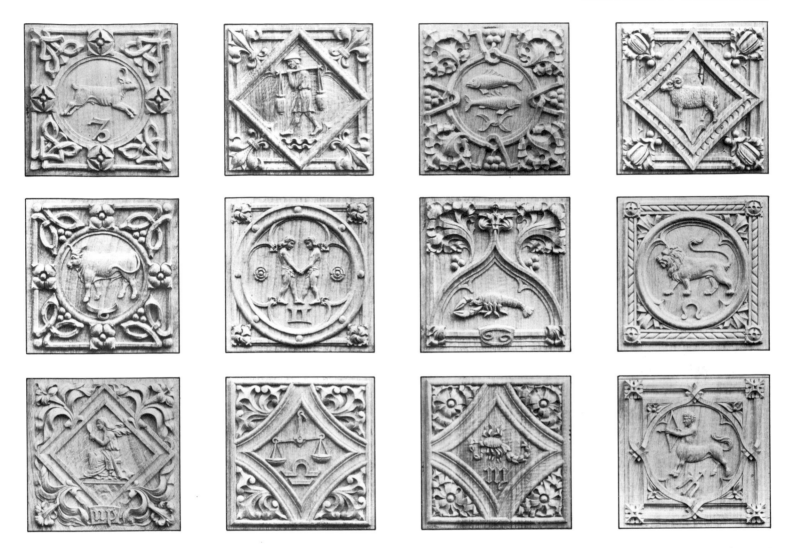

The Signs of the Zodiac. *An indication of the quality of Hahn's designs. The carvings were carried out by a Bristol man Arthur Bird.*

The Grotesques. *The lady and the student with headphones seem curiously prescient of the 1980s. The grotesques were designed by Hahn and were carried out by Bristol carvers Arthur Bird, William Smith and an Italian, Agostini.*

Memorial Building and in the Physics laboratory, he insisted on bronze window frames to avoid corrosion; all rooms to be perhaps two feet higher than thought necessary at the moment of design in case new equipment needed to be acquired which did not fit the present dimensions; all partition walls, although adjustable if required, to be built of the best brick with mortar; Keen's cement plaster to be used everywhere because it did not flake like lime; supply cables not to run along walls because they collect dust but to run in recessed floor channels made easily accessible under unshrinking teak covers; and finally any floor in the laboratory to be rigid enough to support running machinery with negligible vibration. He also saw to it that buildings erected at his cost were given substantial funds to provide for their maintenance. His buildings cost many thousands of pounds to build but they have also saved thousands of pounds in running costs by the excellence of their construction.

If Treasurers, Chairmen of General Purposes Committees, Bursars and Finance Officers have reason to feel grateful to Harry and George Wills for their care in erecting buildings, generations of staff and students must feel grateful too for their purchases. The purchase of the Tyndall's Park estate and Royal Fort House from the trustees of the Tyndall family provided a much-needed space for expansion. The present and future generations must be grateful to Tyndall the professor that the Physics laboratory was built, not on the Repton garden, but on the old stable block and orchard.

The survival of the Goldney gardens was also due to a member of staff. George Wills bought Goldney with the intention of building a men's hall of residence there. According to tradition, Miss Staveley, whose Clifton Hill girls were just across the road, objected on moral grounds and threatened to resign. The minutes of Council show that she had the support of Lloyd Morgan. Harry Wills was all for allowing Miss Staveley to resign but in the end he bought an estate at Downside in Stoke Bishop and, after Harry's death, George built a men's hall there as a memorial to him. Harry's widow, Dame Monica, added a small chapel. Oatley was again the architect and this quasi-Oxbridge college hall and the Dame Monica Wills Chapel alongside rank among his best works. They are certainly better architecture and more pleasant places for their purposes than any of the four other University residences on the site (Churchill 1956, Hiatt Baker 1964, Badock 1964 and University Close 1972).

Balked of his desire to build a hall of residence, Sir George Wills decided to live at Goldney himself. On his death it passed to his daughter Mrs Eberle and when she in turn died it passed to the University with the stipulation that nothing should be done to alter radically the character of the house. But Goldney is only part of the legacy of fine houses that the Wills family conferred upon the University.

The Dame Monica Wills Chapel.

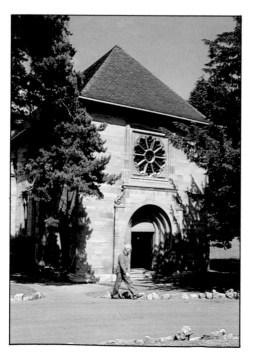

The Founder's Window. *The design for the stained glass. The window was destroyed by enemy action.*

Founders' Window. *When the window was restored it recognised all who had contributed to the founding of the University.*

Burwalls. *Designed by Frank Wills and the home of George Wills it became the University's Short Course Centre after an honourable career as a hall of residence.*

Harry Wills gave Mortimer House (1922) as a hall of residence for men (now a hospital for alcoholics after a period as a maternity hospital). In 1946 Mortimer House was replaced by another home of Sir George when Burwalls (built in 1872) became a men's hall. In Sir George's time, Burwalls was the scene of a unique ceremony. The University of Oxford, like most universities, confers honorary degrees on persons of distinction. Occasionally, if the person to be honoured is ill the degree is conferred *in absentia*. However, when Oxford decided to honour George Wills for his services to higher education, the University, exercising an obscure right it enjoys under Laudian statutes, travelled to confer the degree upon him in his own home. Bristol inherited Burwalls in a poor state. Army occupation during the war had damaged the balustrade, and the steam organ, which once occupied the pleasantly decorated Music Room, was transferred to Malmesbury Abbey. In 1973 Burwalls became the home of the University's Short Course Centre, displaced from Rodney Lodge, the home of P. J. Worsley, one of the founders of both the University College and the University.

In 1959 Captain Douglas Wills gave Bracken Hill, his father Melville Wills' house, to the University to serve as a horticultural centre. Its 5¼ acres not only serve as the University's botanic garden, the lineal descendant of Leipner's Woodland Road garden, but also provide a location for the re-sited

Goldney. *The gardens are full of delightful prospects.*

Goldney Grotto.

Canynge Hall *in an earlier use.*

The Hiatt Baker Memorial Garden.
Established originally on the site now occupied by Senate House, the Hiatt Baker Garden was moved to Bracken Hill. One of the delights of the garden was a little statue of a fawn which, sadly, has been removed by vandals.

Hiatt Baker Memorial Garden, displaced when Senate House was erected in Tyndall Avenue.

Not all the Wills gifts were distinguished buildings. Canynge Hall, given by Harry Wills as a men's hall in 1919, is rather unlovely. Built as a hotel to serve the North Atlantic trade through Clifton Down Station and Avonmouth, it was placed too close to the railway. It was also unfortunately close to a major dairy. A combination of early morning trains and milk bottles proved too much for hotel guests and students alike. The students transferred to Wills Hall in 1929 and Canynge Hall took on a much more useful role as the home of the University's Public Health Department (now the Department of Epidemiology and Community Medicine).

The Victoria Rooms too, despite their splendid classical facade, are somewhat disappointing in their internal arrangements. The foundation stone was laid on 24 May 1828 and the building took four years and £28,000 to erect to a design by Charles Dyer. It is a good example of the 'Greek revival' movement in architecture and its tympanum sculpture *The Advent of Morning* by the then youthful sculptor Jabez Tyley, depicting "Minerva in a biga, driven by Apollo, preceded by the Hours and attended by the Graces", is particularly good. For a little less than a hundred years it was used for a variety of purposes, with visits by Kings, Queens, Prime Ministers and politicians, as well as the notorious Lola Montez and the famous Charles Dickens. It was one of the first buildings in Bristol to be electrically lighted and was also the scene of some early experiments in radio control (before the days of broadcasting) when small airships directed from the stage floated around the hall. Its major feature then was a marvellous organ built originally for 'The Royal Panopticon of Science and Arts, Leicester Square'. This huge instrument had three sets of keyboards playable by three independent organists and contained the first set of drums ever known in organ building. It had been transferred first to St Paul's Cathedral before coming to Bristol, but sadly it was destroyed, together with most of Dyer's interior, in a disastrous fire in 1934. The present interior which "shows a unified design in harmony with the style of the original building, yet expressing the spirit of today", was the work of the Bristol partnership of Gordon Hake and Eustace Button. It worked well as a Union and was clearly liked by generations of students, but its present adaptation as a Physical Education centre and a hall for performing arts is clearly an unhappy compromise: the Victoria Rooms represents both a challenge and an opportunity for the University in the future.

The effect on the University buildings of the Wills family did not end with the deaths of Harry and George Wills. As we have seen, in more recent days Captain Douglas Wills continued their tradition of generous gifts. But the Wills brothers affected the University in other ways. The interest of the Harry Wills Benefaction paid for the building of Manor Hall, another elegant

Victoria Rooms. *Dyer's splendid interior was destroyed by fire in the 1930s but the delightful sculptural work in the tympanum and on the fountain remain.*

The Architecture of Physics. *A combination of Oatley and the Wills brothers was followed less successfully by a partnership between the UGC and Brentnall.*

design by George Oatley. The Wills Benefaction might have produced more such buildings from Oatley, then at the height of his powers, if Stanley Badock had followed the advice of Andrew Robertson to "build during a recession". Badock, however, was reluctant to use the capital funds and preferred to wait for the interest to accumulate before initiating a new project.

It is debatable whether Robertson or Badock was correct. It would have been cheaper to build when Robertson suggested and the result might have been new Engineering, Science and Medical buildings to set alongside Physics (and perhaps to stimulate these disciplines as Physics was by the space and excellence of the accommodation). However, the sites needed might have destroyed the Royal Fort and its garden and given Bristol the technological emphasis in its subjects which characterises Leeds and other universities that continued fast development in the 1930s. At any rate, when the Second World War ended and the years of expansion began, the Wills funds were no longer adequate for major buildings. The Government, through the University Grants Committee, was now the source of building funds, but the UGC 'norms' proved to be less productive of impressive architecture than the philanthropy of the Wills brothers.

Yet in the early years at least, Ralph Brentnall, Oatley's last partner and his successor as the University's favoured architect, managed to continue the Wills and Oatley tradition of quality workmanship, good materials, and low maintenance design. It is fashionable now among architects to deride his contributions to the University's built environment and it is true that some of his major buildings are bland and rather unexciting to look at. The Queen's Building was jointly conceived with Oatley, who wanted a stone finish. Had this been done, embellished and detailed in Oatley's familiar manner, it might have been an ornament to the hillside. As it is, many will agree with Gill's dismissive description "there is size without grandeur". In fairness to Brentnall, however, it must be remembered that he managed to keep up a high standard of interior finish despite the financial restrictions imposed by the UGC and the physical constraints, particularly in the case of the Medical School, of local government planning restrictions.

Brentnall's other major contributions, the Physics extension and Senate House, built under UGC constraints, are no worse than many buildings of the period erected elsewhere in the city without regard to cost; they are similar too, and in detail possibly better than, other buildings erected under UGC patronage in other universities. Brentnall also showed himself to be clever and resourceful in adaptations. His refectory within the old city Art Gallery is pleasant, but his extension to the Wills Memorial Building library was remarkable in that few people now remember that it was extended. The University owes him a debt too for his meticulous rebuilding of the Great Hall, a seven year task made possible by the foresight and generosity of another Wills, Lord Dulverton, who purchased prime English oak for the task soon after the 1941 air-raid which destroyed it. When the original contractors, Henry Willcocks, began the task of rebuilding in 1948 the timber was seasoned and ready for the carpenters and joiners, some of whom had worked on the original Great Hall as apprentices and had returned to undertake the restoration.

Bristolians are in Brentnall's debt too for his careful rebuilding of St Michael's Hill in the 1960s. Conservation was not then the accepted doctrine it is today and Brentnall's meticulous use of hundreds of photographs to recreate the original houses which, when the University acquired them, were close to collapse, was an object lesson to many who, in later years, suddenly discovered the architectural merits of old buildings. He was not an architect who saw his projects as a way to achieve his own immortality. He believed in building in the interests of his clients, in the best available materials used with the highest degree of skill. He lacked the flair and wit of Oatley but in everything else he was a worthy pupil of his old master and partner.

None of the architects who followed Brentnall has exhibited a strong individual signature. The Courtaulds Group's Chemistry building is an imposing building in the international modern style which has coped well with a difficult site. Its decorative detail is over-busy and other features, such as the cantilevered lecture theatre, seem the product of fashion rather than an individual response to a challenge. Universities and other major public buildings elsewhere in the country are similarly blessed. In the case of its wide open piazza with fountain – the product of misplaced optimism about the British climate – it is cursed as places elsewhere are.

Twist and Whitley's main Library building is curiously unassertive although it is prominently placed at the crest of St Michael's Hill. Its internal arrangements and finishes are excellent and it deserves not only the gratitude of its users, the readers, but the wider recognition given to it by an award from the Library Association. However, it is not a unique building. It is very like the same architects' Science Library at Belfast which on the whole is more successful because its unprepossessing exterior is hidden by trees and a terrace of Victorian houses.

Michael Grice's flats at Goldney also deserved the award they received from the Civic Trust. Grice's firm, the Architects Co-Partnership, was responsible for the much-criticised tower blocks at Essex University – but while his Goldney residences have much the same idiom their scale is less and their very modern grey concrete blends remarkably well at close quarters with the eighteenth century garden and at a distance with the Clifton townscape in which they can be seen. Since their construction they have proved to be the most popular residences available to students.

One of the University's most recent buildings, an extension to Rodney Lodge for the School for Advanced Urban Studies, also won an award.

St Michael's Hill. *The University's careful rebuilding created a fine street out of slums.*

Restoration. *Bligh Bond's old medical building was restored after a disastrous fire in the Geography Department. The Lord Mayor and Lady Mayoress of Bristol and Dr Richard Hill, Chairman of the University Council, chat with Professor Peter Haggett, Acting Vice-Chancellor (1984–85) at the re-opening.*

Rodney Lodge. *In the main Georgian building at Rodney Lodge there are some reminders of its former use – in particular a fine Wedgwood fireplace.*

Powell and Moya, the architects for the Festival of Britain exhibition site, were asked to build teaching, library and residential accommodation in a sensitive part of the Clifton Conservation area. The resulting building, a restrained two-storey structure, has not much character and some believe it represents a wasted opportunity. However the staff who use it like it and the RIBA were sufficiently impressed to award it a Commendation.

Another University building (in the course of construction in 1984) may also attract an award. It is Richard MacCormac's ambitious combination of a conservation scheme and a new lineal building for the Arts Faculty in Woodland Road. The Victorian houses involved in the scheme were solidly built (one of them was the home of the Sturge family who were among the founders and the first students of the University College). Some years earlier Eustace Button demonstrated what could be done by linking three of them by bridges at the first floor level. MacCormac's scheme extends this link along the rear of the houses on an elevated walkway which surmounts the roofs of additional staff rooms, teaching rooms, and common rooms built as pavilions in the gardens of the villas. Some may feel that the pavilions, particularly in the common rooms, have a style reminiscent of the 1950s – a mixture of coffee-bar with early Habitat – but the staff who work in the first phases of the building confess themselves delighted with their accommodation, and the return of these houses to something like their former appearance after many years of misuse by Government departments and public utilities is welcomed by conservationists.

A feature of the Woodland Road Development is the little courts and gardens which the L-shaped nature of the pavilions creates. Their presence represents continuing optimism; the history of such courts and gardens in previous University buildings is a sad one. As the University's need for accommodation has not always been matched by its ability to pay for new buildings, resourceful academics have cast their eyes on the open spaces. All over the University there is evidence of in-filling and improvisation. In recent years the University has managed to push back this tide of temporary buildings (the earliest of which goes back to 1878) when it created a garden, called the Centenary Garden, by demolishing a prefabricated hut which had served usefully as an employees' club but completely ruined the Royal Fort gardens in which it was located.

The University has also shown a capacity to adapt buildings with great ingenuity. The Department of Geography has redesigned the space inside the envelope of the Hansom and Bligh Bond buildings in University Road. The Employees' Club, displaced from their garden hut, now has a bar, a skittle alley and billiard rooms below the Cecil Powell Centre for Science Education in converted commercial premises in Old Park Hill. Perhaps the most interesting adaptations of this kind have been those for the Drama Department. In 1951 a disused squash rackets court at the rear of the Wills Memorial Building was converted into a studio. In 1966 the Vandyck Printers' buildings were converted to provide a Studio Theatre (now called the Glynne Wickham Studio Theatre), classrooms, staffrooms, workshops and accommodation for the Theatre Collection, which is still the only fully catalogued major theatre collection in Britain.

But even if the Drama Department (and its associated television and radio facilities) represent the most interesting adaptations, the most successful and most beautiful changes of use must be the University's Georgian houses. Bristol has more listed buildings than Bath, its neighbouring Georgian city, and it is appropriate that Bristol's University should have, and care for, some splendid examples of the Georgian house builders' art. The best examples are certainly Royal Fort House and Clifton Hill but Cliftonwood House, Richmond House, Goldney (despite Alfred Waterhouse's Victorian additions), Rodney Lodge (despite an additional storey added by Worsley) and in former days Mortimer House, have many incidental felicities – doorways, fireplaces, early mouldings and plasterwork – which delight the eye and the mind. At Royal Fort the chief delight within Bridges' overall design is the plaster and carving produced by Thomas Paty. Paty was also a major contributor with Samuel Glascodine, the carpenter, and Joseph Thomas, the tiler and plasterer, to Clifton Hill. Built in 1747 for Paul Fisher, a founder of the Bristol Royal Infirmary, Clifton Hill was afterwards the

Another Award-winner? *One of the new pavilions in the Woodland Road Arts Building.*

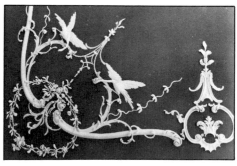

Royal Fort House. *Formerly the home of the Tyndall family, it served the University first as the Men's Union, then as the Department of Education. Its present users, the Department of Music, no doubt please the ghost of the lady which is supposed to haunt the first floor.*

The Tyndall Family. *One of the few reminders of the family which still remain in the house.*

Clifton Hill the University's first hall of residence. Clifton Manor House, Richmond House, Rivers Cottage and other properties joined it as annexes. In the 1960s it was extended.

Hercules in winter at Goldney. His companion Bacchus disappeared some time in the last century.

home of John Addington Symonds, one of the first physicians appointed by the General Hospital. His son, of the same name, was an early supporter of the University College and the Committee for 'the Higher Education of Women'. The decision to buy it to serve as the University's first hall of residence was taken across the road at Goldney, then the home of Lewis Fry.

The treasure of Clifton Hill is also partly in its furnishings. Miss Staveley and her assistant Miss Barry bought antiques with impeccable taste and sometimes from their own pockets. The Addington Symonds family have contributed books and other material and Mrs Henly Evans arranged the return of the lead dolphin which decorated the pond in the garden. The Wills family – in particular Sir George, Mrs Hilda Wills, and Jean, Lady Wills, were also generous in their support.

It is sad that the rich furniture of the Tyndall family was sold before Harry Wills bought Royal Fort House: only one fine portrait of the family about to play cricket can definitely be associated with the original family. Goldney fortunately still retains its glory, the Grotto created by Thomas Goldney over a period of 17 years from the exotic sea shells brought home to him by Bristol's sea captains. The tower which supplies the water for the cascade and the canal also survive in their original condition and setting. Goldney's statue of Hercules continues to swing his club on the lawns but of an accompanying statue of Bacchus there is now no trace.

Of course, Goldney Grotto, though it is one of the University's, and indeed the city's major treasures, is only part of a living, developing institution. The University's buildings are certainly varied, ranging in age from the mid-eighteenth century to the late twentieth. Its architects have sometimes been strange choices: who would have predicted that the Quakers and Non-Conformists who dominated the University College Council would, at a time of strong doctrinal divisions, have chosen a Catholic architect like Hansom? Who would have thought that an underprivileged orphan boy from St Paul's through the unlikely agency of a phrenologist would become an architect and, as Sir George Oatley, create his city's finest building? Who would have believed that a bomb disposal expert, seriously wounded defusing an enemy charge, would live to become Oatley's junior partner in the firm of Oatley and Brentnall and his successor as the University's chosen architect?

It is certainly easy to be critical of many of the buildings the University has acquired since the Charter was granted 75 years ago or which it inherited at that time. They are indeed a mixed stock and views about them differ. For Gill, the symbolic Wills Memorial Building was "a sham"; for one contemporary writing on the occasion of its opening its external armorials resembled (appropriately) cigarette cards. For others, Oatley's work seems timeless while that of his most recent successors already looks inept and dated. But in Bristol University's rich and eclectic range of buildings there is something for every taste and perhaps this is how a university should be in its physical-built environment, not a conspicuous adherent of any one school of thought, but embracing and exemplifying all.

Space Problems. *Academic staff seeking new facilities have a way of expanding into open spaces.*

Chapter Ten

Looking Forward

In its petition to the King seeking a Charter, the University College Council humbly submitted that "the creation of a University of Bristol is urgently called for in order to enable the inhabitants of the city and its neighbourhood to obtain such educational advantages as have resulted from the establishment of universities in the large commercial cities in Europe and America". The petition of the citizens (in fact the University Committee set up by Lewis Fry) was somewhat more provincial in its humble submission. "By the creation of a University of Bristol", the Lord Mayor Edward B. James and 88 other signatories said, "a great benefit will be conferred on the inhabitants of that city and western counties enabling them to obtain such educational and other advantages as have resulted from the establishment of universities in Manchester, Birmingham, Liverpool, Leeds and Sheffield".

In 1925, in a booklet produced to mark the occasion of the opening of the Wills Memorial Building, F. W. Rixon changed the target of emulation to the older universities. There is something which happens to a man as a result of training in certain centres, he asserted. "It is a flavour that clings throughout life; it pervades thought, it shapes conduct, it modifies behaviour; it is an ethereal philosophy so strong that it is inescapable and yet so frail that it must be guarded with all care. How it comes is not known . . . Oxford and Cambridge have it . . . can we look for the day when a man, asked for his University, will say, with equal pride, "Bristol"?"

Rixon answered his own question, "It is coming! A city proud of its university, a university proud of its home, every member a stone in a building, thrilled with the thought of the unutterable grandeur of the whole".

By the time the 50th anniversary of the Charter came around, however, Bristol was sufficiently self-confident to speak of the future in terms of its own history and example. It was proud of its expansion. "The University", wrote Sir Philip Morris, "is well aware of the dangers of mere size. Its development so far has indeed been in response to demand but this demand has not come only from the numbers hammering at its gates. It has been an organic growth diversified by new developments and disciplines and there is

no reason to believe that the pattern of future development will belie the past. The interests of each Faculty widen and deepen with the receding horizons of knowledge and in each new interest put down roots and mature into new departments and schools." Sir Philip could see a clear direction for the University to take for the future. "The aim of all of us will be to conserve and develop the best elements of the University we have known and to maintain that individuality and character which has exercised such an influence over all its members, past and present."

In 1959 it was possible to see the future not only clearly but with optimism; in 1984, on the occasion of the 75th anniversary of the Charter, confident prognosis was much more difficult. In the early part of that year the Government and the universities conducted an anxious dialogue about the years to the end of the century, the agenda decided by a letter from the Chairman of the UGC, Sir Peter Swinnerton-Dyer. In his letter Sir Peter listed 28 questions to which the UGC, and beyond the Committee the Government, wanted answers. They dealt with such matters as funding of universities, entrance requirements and relationships between the universities and the polytechnics. The attitudes behind the questions were sometimes more interesting than the questions themselves. Some revealed the curious tenacity of Bryce's idea of the 'examining university' when they suggested that the self-regulating system sanctioned by external examiners of the

Degree Congregation. *The outward and continuing sign of autonomy conveyed by the Charter – the conferring of the University's own degrees.*

The City of Bristol. *The role played by the City in obtaining the Charter is reflected in the Lord Mayor's annual attendance at degree congregations.*

147

Honorary Degrees. *The University honours itself by honouring people prominent in the city, national and international life. The Vice-Chancellor Sir Alec Merrison with Bristol philanthropist John James.*

autonomous 'Haldane' universities might be abandoned in favour of a new version of the CNAA. Others queried the value that should be attached to the idea of 'tenure' – which many University members saw as central to the idea of an autonomous university controlled in its academic affairs by its own Senate. And universities were also required to think about the importance of student choice of course or, as the Germans call it, *Lernfreiheit*. The whole letter appeared to be imbued with a spirit of gloom. The Government evidently saw a future of declining student numbers and economic difficulty in which some universities, and certainly some university departments, might have to close.

Bristol, in its Senate and Council debates, firmly rejected what it described as "this limply defeatist attitude". In a trenchantly worded letter it set out its views of its own future and the future of university education in the nation. It stated its belief that nationally there would be no decline in the numbers of students seeking a university education; for its own part, Bristol foresaw that it would continue to attract large numbers of well-qualified applicants for places. It saw itself not as a large university but as a university which had a large and varied spread of subjects, a richness of disciplines. In what one professor in Senate's debate on the University's reply to the Swinnerton-Dyer letter described as a "proper, confident, robust, *Bristol* response", the University outlined the difficulties it wanted to overcome and the opportunities it wanted to seize.

The difficulties it identified flowed mainly from the cuts of 1981. The effect of losing even one member of staff on the smaller 'arts-based' departments had been disproportionately harmful; the University wanted these to be strengthened as an immediate priority. The technical, secretarial and clerical support for academic staff also needed to be strengthened. Clinical Medicine and Dentistry were under-funded and had not been given any protection by the UGC from the July 1981 cuts. To fund these and other development the University told the UGC it would need more, not less, resources. And the University made clear it did not only need money: it needed space. Although the University had sold off some of its properties after the 1981 cuts in a bid to rationalise its accommodation by 1984, it believed that more space would be needed to allow Engineering, Computer Science, Information Technology, Molecular Genetics and other academic growth points to develop properly.

The growth of these areas was one of the opportunities the University wanted to seize. The University believed that experience in Information Technology would become an important part of 'arts' as well as 'science' skills. This bridging of the gap between 'the two cultures', as C. P. Snow described it, should be reflected in the development of cross-Faculty degree courses. Bristol had had some courses of this kind; the Joint School of Geology and Archaeology was probably unique in the country, but in the spring of 1984 it seemed to Senate that there was an opportunity for further development. The non-examinable 'Engineer in Society' course in which young engineers (in an unconscious fulfilment of the ideas of Percival and Jowett) had been confronted with disciplines such as Law, Accountancy and Sociology could be developed into Joint Schools of Engineering with Economics or Engineering with a Language. Alternatively, there seemed opportunities to combine Economics with a natural science.

To some older members of the University the discussion of these topics may have recalled an attempt Bristol made in the 1960s to pioneer management studies at Rodney Lodge. After some years' experimentation, Bristol decided then to leave business education to London and Manchester (where Bristol's Professor Stanley Kent had gone in the 1920s to start a department which was a very early attempt to combine science with management). But the situation in the 1980s was different. The School for Advanced Urban Studies had shown a capacity to run satisfactory courses of a post-experience kind in policy studies. On a much wider front, both geographically and academically, the Department of Extra-Mural Studies was fulfilling all Haldane's hopes for extension studies and the founders' ideas of spreading 'the University experience' throughout the five surrounding counties. In some medical areas of continuing education, as extension of University work was now called, the influence and teaching of the University spread as far west as the Scilly Isles. Western England, to adapt Jowett's phrase, was being "inoculated with Bristol".

In 1984 the University drew all this continuing education work under one body for the first time, an executive committee chaired by a Pro-Vice-Chancellor. The idea was to create a structure in which it could expand and develop. The same attempt to draw together interesting developing areas also manifested itself elsewhere within the University. Work in Molecular Genetics, making good progress in a range of departments, was drawn together in a special unit headed by Professor J. E. Beringer and other departments contributed from their varying perspectives to the development of information technology.

In several other disciplines it was possible to distinguish common interests which might lead to fruitful co-operation between departments and even, in time, the possible growth of a new subject. For example, the Physics Department established links with Long Ashton in food technology. The physicists' long-term interest in the physics of materials was parallelled by Chemistry's and Engineering's interest in polymers, in fluid mechanics and the possibilities of new engineering materials. Economics and environmental concerns attracted the attention of Geography (especially with its new Remote Sensing Unit), Chemistry and the Biological Science Departments. On the medical side, the immunological approach to cancer, particularly viral cancers, characterised the work of several departments. In 1983 this

Remote Sensing. *The Remote Sensing Unit in Geography uses space pictures to predict,* inter alia, *where locusts will swarm. This is Bristol.*

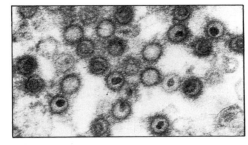

EB virus. *A cancer-causing virus, the first to be discovered, was found by Professor Epstein and his research assistant, Yvonne Barr. The Epstein-Barr (EB) virus, related to the herpes simplex virus, causes cancer of the nose and throat and may be implicated in other diseases. A prototype vaccine, developed by Professor Epstein, was tested first in 1983.*

New Vice-Chancellor *Professor John Kingman, appointed to succeed Sir Alec Merrison and become the University's next Vice-Chancellor.*

continuing interest of Bristol researchers reached a notable milestone when Professor Epstein was able to announce the discovery of a prototype vaccine against Burkitt's Lymphoma and virally caused cancers of the ears, nose and throat. Interest in the psychology of learning, language and perception bridged the Medical, Education, Social Sciences and Science Faculties.

While it was possible to distinguish these linkages, and it was also possible to identify areas of traditional strength in the University, no-one could say with certainty that it was from such areas that the most interesting and significant new developments for the future would appear. Events which seem trivial to those who participate in them often acquire significance only with hindsight: just as Tyndall's proposal for a new battery room led to the building of the Wills Physics Laboratory, so too a minor request already made and met might in time be seen as the seed from which great things have grown. It is the random combination of factors which often determines the most 'exciting developments.

Yet universities plan for the future – the University's response to the Swinnerton-Dyer letter can be seen as one such plan – and they can make other dispositions. In December 1983, Bristol was able to announce that, after a period in which Professor Peter Haggett would be Acting Vice-Chancellor, Sir Alec Merrison would be succeeded in 1985 as Vice-Chancellor by the Chairman of the Science and Engineering Research Council, the distinguished mathematician, Professor John Kingman. Professor Kingman resembled some of his predecessors in that he was young at the time of his appointment and had already established a brilliant reputation as a scholar and administrator. But in one respect he was unlike them. In that respect he could be seen as the fulfilment of the hopes of the founders; for it was a hope of Jowett, Percival and their friends that one day the College they founded would draw its professors and indeed its chief academic officer from Oxford or Cambridge. For many years the University College was too poor to attract such a candidate. For some years after the Charter the new University of Bristol lacked the academic reputation to excite the interest of Oxbridge applicants for the Vice-Chancellorship. It has always chosen men of distinction as Vice-Chancellor but not, as it happened, men who were at the time of their appointment associated with either of the two older universities. Professor Kingman's acceptance of the invitation to become Vice-Chancellor can therefore be seen as another sign that Bristol's University has fulfilled the hopes of its founders.

A University celebrating the 75th anniversary of its Charter looks for and is gladdened by such signs. Tradition means more in uncertain times, and the Bristol staff and students of today and of the future are the inheritors of no mean tradition. In following tradition academically, they can hope to be, in Ramsay's words, "A faculty that loves learning and wisdom". They can fulfil a role in the state and in the local community; and thus they can be members of, in Haldane's favourite phrase, "a provincial Charlottenberg". They can attach themselves to the principles of *Lehrfreiheit* and *Lernfreiheit* of the German tradition. They can uphold the Scottish tradition of the Charter, of Sonnenschein of Birmingham and Murray of Liverpool, "a faculty-run University with a strong Senate". They can be true to Morris' vision by rejecting "capitulation to the insistent demands of the immediate present" and by generating "the ideas that are needed to sustain a free, responsible society". And in a future in which Government and public may doubt the value of universities, they can justify themselves, as Merrison would wish them to do, by being supremely good at what universities do best – scholarship.

And if such traditions seem at times a little too solemn too sententious to live up to, there are other minor traditions to follow. One thinks of Chattock, who used his knowledge of electricity to provide the lights (the first electric lights on the English stage) for the fairies on the first night of Gilbert and Sullivan's *Iolanthe*. One remembers Piper who, discovering a boy student kissing a girl student in the laboratory one evening, said quietly, "I think you would do well to remember that the right to demonstrate in this laboratory is confined to the staff". One recalls the redoubtable Dr Millicent Taylor calmly instructing student fire-watchers during the Second World War, the route by which, should the structure be on fire, the Wills Memorial Building might be safely descended – on the outside.

A University which faces even an uncertain future with such courage and skill, humour and discipline, scholarship and ingenuity should fear no problems of survival. In the future the University of Bristol will continue, in the words of the humble submission to King Edward, to provide "the educational and other advantages which have resulted from the establishment of universities in Manchester, Birmingham, Liverpool, Leeds and Sheffield, . . . and, in the large cities in Europe and America". Bristol is now, and seems likely to continue to be, a national centre of teaching and scholarship with an international reputation. In the years ahead Bristol hopes to welcome more overseas students, and its research programmes already draw support not only from Britain but from major companies and government and charitable agencies in Europe and America. From the original modest aim of serving the youth and industry of one city the University now has assumed world-wide responsibilities. But its international obligations will not make it forget its duties to its region and its city, for it is, in H. O. Wills', its first Chancellor's phrase, "A university for Bristol", and a university of which Bristol can be proud.

Chattock's Fairies. *Pictured on the front page of a piece of popular music, the lights devised by Chattock show clearly. This was the first use of electric light on the English stage. Later in* Iolanthe's *run all the fairies were given lights.*

Bibliography

ALLUM, R., *The University Sheffield Made*, Gazette No.59, Sheffield, University of Sheffield, 1978.

Alumni Gazette, Bristol, University of Bristol, Annual Series.

ANONYMOUS, *University of Bristol 1925*, Bristol, J. W. Arrowsmith, 1925.

ASHBY, Eric & ANDERSON, Mary, *Portrait of Haldane*, London, Macmillan, 1974. *The Rise of the Student Estate in Britain*, London, Macmillan, 1974.

ASHBY, Eric, *University College, Liverpool and Three Scotsmen*, (unpublished public lecture typescript), Liverpool, University of Liverpool, 1978.

Minutes of the Education Committee, Bristol, City and County of Bristol, 1930-1939.

BROTHERS, J. & HATCH, S., *Residence and Student Life*, London, Tavistock, 1971.

BUTCHER, E. E., *Clifton Hill House – The First Phase 1909–1959*, Bristol, University of Bristol, undated.

CHAPMAN, A. W., *The Story of a Modern University* (History of the University of Sheffield), Oxford, Oxford University Press, 1955.

University Charter (University College Bristol Petition. Petition of Bristol Citizens. Charter of Incorporation.), Bristol, Benson, Carpenter, Cross and Williams (Solicitors), 1909.

CHEESEWRIGHT, M., *Mirror to a Mermaid*, Birmingham, University of Birmingham, 1975.

City and County of Bristol, *Minutes of the Education Committee*, 1930-1939.

COTTLE, B. & SHERBORNE, J. W., *The Life of a University*, Bristol, University of Bristol, 1959.

'FLAMBEAU', OATLEY, G. & RIXON, F. W. (Contributors), *Bristol University*, Bristol, Partridge and Love, 1925.

FLEXNER, A., *Universities: American, English, German*, New York, Oxford University Press, 1930.

GEDDES, Sir Patrick, *Report to Council*, Bristol, University of Bristol Library Special Collection.

GOSDEN, P. H. J. H. & TAYLOR, A. J. (Eds.), *Studies in the History of a University 1874–1974*, Leeds, Arnold, 1975.

GREIG, James, *Silvanus P. Thompson – Teacher*, London, HMSO, 1979.

HOWARTH, T. E. B., *Cambridge between Two Wars* London, Collins, 1978.

HUMPHREYS, D. W., *The University of Bristol and the Education and Training of Teachers*, Bristol, University of Bristol School of Education, 1976.

JONES, R. V., *Most Secret War*, London, Hamilton, 1978.

KELSALL, R. K., *Applications for Admission to Universities*, London, CVCP, 1957.

KENT, F. L., *The University of Bristol Library*, The Journal of Documentation No.3, Vol.5, 1949.

LEONARD, G. H., *Some Memories of John Addington Symonds and Clifton Hill House*, Bristol, University of Bristol, undated.

MacQUEEN, J. G. & TAYLOR, S. W. (Eds.), *University and Community*, Bristol, University of Bristol, 1976.

McGRATH, Patrick, *The Merchant Venturers of Bristol*, Bristol, The Society of Merchant Venturers, 1975.

MARSHALL, Mary Paley, *What I Remember*, Cambridge, Cambridge University Press, 1947.

MELLER, H. E., *Leisure and the Changing City*, London, Routledge and Kegan Paul, 1976.

MOODIE, G. & EUSTACE, R., *Power and Authority in British Universities*, London, Allen and Unwin, 1974.

MOODY, T. W. & BECKETT, J. C., *The Queen's University of Belfast 1845–1949*, London, Faber and Faber, 1959.

MORRIS, Jan, *The Oxford Book of Oxford*, Oxford, Oxford University Press, 1978.

Newsletter; Bristol, University of Bristol, Vols 1-14, 1970-1984.

PERRY, C. Bruce, *The Bristol Royal Infirmary*, Bristol, Portishead Press, 1981.

PHILLIPSON, N. (Ed.), *Universities, Society and the Future*, Edinburgh, Edinburgh University Press, 1983.

PIKE, D. J. & GARDNER, J. M., *Neighbourhood Universities*, Reading, University of Reading, 1975.

Robbins Report, Command 2154, London, HMSO, 1963.

ROBBINS, Lord, *The University in the Wider World*, London, Macmillan, 1966.

ROME, Alan, *George Oatley*, (unpublished public lecture typescript), Bristol, University of Bristol, 1976.

SANDERSON, M., *The Universities and British Industry*, London, Routledge and Kegan Paul, 1972.

SHERBORNE, James, *University College Bristol 1876–1909* (Frederick Creech Jones Memorial Lecture), Bristol, Bristol Historical Association, 1976.

SMITHERS, Alan G., *Sandwich Courses*, London, NFER, 1976.

THOMPSON, Jane Smeal & THOMPSON, Helen G., *Silvanus Phillips Thompson – His Life and Letters*, London, T. Fisher Unwin, 1920.

TRAVERS, Morris, *Autobiography*, (unpublished typescript MS228), London, University College London Library, 1976. *Letters and Notes*, (Box 84, Ramsay Collection), London, University College London Library. *Sir William Ramsay*, London, Arnold, 1956.

TYNDALL, A. M., *Letters, notes etc.*, Bristol, University of Bristol Library Special Collection.

The Governors of the United Bristol Hospitals with the University of Bristol, *The University of Bristol Dental School and Hospital*, Bristol, 1964.

WEBER, R. I., *Pioneers of Science*, London and Bristol, Institute of Physics, 1980.

WILLIAMS, G., BLACKSTONE, T. & METCALF, D., *The Academic Labour Market*, Amsterdam, Elsevier, 1974.

WILSON, Roger, *Sir Philip Morris* (A memorial address), Bristol, University of Bristol, 1980.

WRIGHT, E. C., *Participation, Disruption and Moderation – An account of recent staff student relations in the University*, Bristol, University of Bristol, 1969.

The Calendars and other official records of the University of Bristol and the University College, Bristol have also been used. The Minutes and records of the University Union, and the files of the student newspapers *Nonesuch, Nonesuch News* and *Bacus* were consulted.